Noted!

Business Lessons Learned from Twenty-Two Years of Virtual Assistance

CHELA HARDY

Published by AskChela LLC
Copyright © 2024 Chela Hardy

Printed in the United States of America

Chela Hardy
Noted! Business Lessons Learned from Twenty-Two Years of Virtual Assistance
ISBN: 979-8-9900239-0-1 (Paperback)
ISBN: 979-8-9900239-1-8 (Ebook)

BUS080000 BUSINESS & ECONOMICS / Home-Based Businesses
BUS115000 BUSINESS & ECONOMICS / Freelance & Self-Employment
BUS020000 BUSINESS & ECONOMICS / Development / Business Development

Cover design: Chela Hardy

AskChela

www.AskChela.com

*To all the Virtual Assistants committed to
making a success of the journey...*

Acknowledgment

Kamili Thom, a talented writer who listened to me talk each lesson through, didn't hesitate to make brilliant suggestions along the way, and was willing to put an eager second set of eyes on my project at just the right intervals. Thank you, my friend!

A Note from Chela

On podcasts and in conversations with my coaching clients and others, I proudly talk about having designed AskChela to allow me plenty of rest and downtime, including a daily nap. I have several chronic issues I've been dealing with (Congestive Heart Failure, Type II Diabetes, Asthma and Depression) for almost as long as I've had my business. Thankfully, I am able to manage these with medication and lifestyle, as long as I pace myself properly.

At the time I began writing this book, I had *not* been pacing myself properly at all. In fact, to settle my nerves at being admitted for what we hoped was not a heart attack, I started scribbling notes for the book from my hospital bed (the first of two occurrences within the same week, the second of which involved Morphine just to deal with the pain. *Morphine!*). It was quite an eventful week, that's for sure. And you can imagine, on top of that, the depression that comes with the feelings of disappointment at not being able to continue with my client work and having to accept that an immediate doctor-recommended medical leave from my business was in order.

Sigh.

Even after many years in business, and even after knowing better, I had let myself burn out.

That was one of the darker teachable moments on my Virtual Assistant journey. But that's not to say that I haven't learned plenty of *good* lessons along the way! And now that I am back in business and back in balance, I have some time on my hands and am excited to share the lessons with you so that you—

- learn from the good and perhaps apply it to your own business and

- steer your way around the not-so-good so you don't end up in a hospital bed feeling sorry for yourself and painfully unsure of what's to come next

To give you a little backstory—

I stumbled into a career as a Virtual Assistant in 2001. While I had always dreamed of someday being an entrepreneur (my father raised us kids with that mindset), I wasn't actually looking to start my business at the time that I did. Circumstances led me to it—a relocation from Connecticut to Northern Virginia at one of the most challenging of economic times. The dotcom bubble had recently burst, and the shiny buildings that lined the well-traveled road along what is known as the Dulles Technology Corridor (near Dulles Airport in Virginia) were suddenly half-filled or nearly empty. The job market had shifted quickly and unexpectedly, and I was not at all prepared for it when I moved.

Even still, I needed to work. So I took my skill set and know-how as a longtime Executive Assistant, called myself a "Freelance Administrative Professional", pitched a few services to small companies in my area, and began to cobble together something that would later come to be known as virtual assistance: working from home on my own equipment supporting small businesses with a set of services they needed taken care of as they continued to deliver their own products and services to their clients and customers.

At the time I started this career path, my *why* was *sheer desperation*. But that's not a sustainable mindset, and it affected the early days of my business in ways that allowed self-doubt to creep in. Eventually, that self-doubt took over completely, and I found myself back in Corporate America doing work I hated, even if I was grateful for it.

Life in Northern Virginia is expensive, so there was always the need for a side hustle to help make ends meet. Virtual assistance was that for me, which upgraded my *why* from *sheer desperation* to *a practical means to an end*. That's a better mindset for sure, though it still wasn't anything to post up on a wall as inspiration. But it kept me in touch with an industry I was excited to watch take shape and form over time. Even then, I could see its potential. I was in and out of Corporate America more than once over the years to follow, but I knew virtual assistance was a career path I wanted to someday jump into in a larger way.

Maintaining a presence in the growing virtual assistance industry while employed full-time was a good move, as it allowed me to make connections along the way, ones that would serve me well years later. Because I had the security of a full-time paycheck, I was able to try out different services in my business and quickly determine which ones I could consistently offer, as well as those I absolutely hated offering.

When I eventually did end up going full-time in my business for the first time, I moved from general virtual assistance to anyone and everyone to offering services specific to creatives, authors, and speakers. It made all the difference! Suddenly, I'd found my place and my voice in this industry. And part of that revelation has emboldened me to teach others what I know as a coach, mentor, workshop facilitator, blogger, occasional speaker—and now an author.

So that's what this book is. A collection of some of the

many things I've noted along the way in my business at both its best and its worst. I've tried to put the lessons in an order and within sections that make sense in my head (with the invaluable help of Kamili from my *Acknowledgments* and her keen second set of eyes and ears):

- Getting Started

- Finding Your Groove

- Making Boss Moves

- Parting Thoughts

At the end of each lesson, you'll find two lined pages where you can briefly note your own take on these lessons. Need more space, a few worksheets, and several writing prompts to help you get the most from what you read? Visit **AskChela.com** to learn about the companion workbook.

My hope is that all of it will successfully move you forward in your business.

You ready? Let's go!

🖤Chela

Table of Contents

Getting Started

Want to set yourself and your business up for success? Use the lessons in this section to get ahead of the learning curve and reach your personal and professional goals sooner.

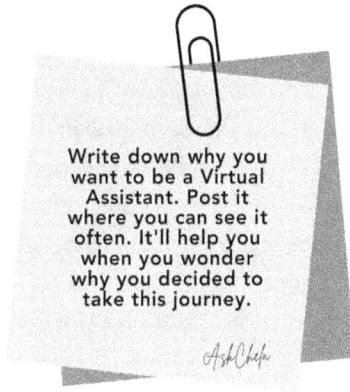

Write down why you want to be a Virtual Assistant. Post it where you can see it often. It'll help you when you wonder why you decided to take this journey.

AskChefa

If you ask ten Virtual Assistants why they started their businesses, you'll likely get ten different responses, though many will likely include some variation-slash-combination of being unhappy in a current job, a need to work from home to resolve challenges related to affordable childcare or caregiving, the desire to cut down on a lengthy commute, sudden unemployment, wanting to spend more time with family, et cetera.

We all have our personal and professional reasons for getting into this industry. And I would venture to say that most come into this with a positive mindset of *yes, I can do this…I can make a success of a career as a Virtual Assistant.* Some go it alone, picking up whatever strategies they can from around the internet and on social media. Some sign up for and take self-paced courses or programs to learn what it takes to start a VA business. Others immediately seek out professional coaching to get ahead of the learning curve and set themselves up for more immediate success. Whatever path they take, they typically have a positive outlook when they begin.

Then reality sets in, and many new VAs realize it's going to be a bit harder than they expected to land clients and bring in the income they need to sustain their business and their financial needs. After a while, some decide that perhaps virtual assistance is not the right career choice for them after all, and they go back and forth about whether to keep going.

This is where remembering their *why* can be helpful. *Why* they decided to pursue this career path. *Why* they felt excited and hopeful about getting started. *Why* they were initially convinced they could make this work—even when family members and friends around them didn't get it, didn't offer up emotional support, or who flat-out refused to believe that a whole segment of the population actually makes their living as VAs.

Is this where you are right now on your journey? Perhaps you're facing a lack of emotional support, or you haven't landed the paying clients you need. Are you thinking of giving up on being a VA? What was your *why* for setting out on this career path? Do you remember?

I hope you've literally written it down and posted it somewhere you can see it easily so that you can quickly call to mind why you said you wanted to do this! And if you haven't already, please do so right now.

Right this very moment.

I'll wait.

In my ebook *Become a More Confident Virtual Assistant*, there's a section on visualizing success. In it, I talk about the power of a good vision board. Honestly, I never gave the concept much weight until I attended an in-person event during which everyone in the room created their own board based on their specific wants, needs, circumstances, et cetera.

Going through the exercise of getting my thoughts out onto something large-sized and tangible was cathartic. Suddenly, I felt empowered at a time when I was doubting myself and my abilities.

So now I teach my coachees and mentees that creating their own vision board can help mute the noise of their negative thoughts. A proper vision board offers a visual representation of the things you want to accomplish in your life in general, but it's also an amazing tool to help you think through and gain clarity on what you want your VA business to look like for you.

Maybe you're wondering just what to put on your board. Don't overthink it! Consider any or all of these things (and anything else that comes to mind and factors into your personal visualization of success):

- Logos of VA organizations you'd like to someday join

- Magazine covers featuring positive VA headlines

- Inspirational quotes from the blogs or social media accounts of some of your favorite VA industry thought leaders

- Screenshots of a few VA colleague websites that give you ideas for creating or refreshing your own business website

- Images of exotic places or getaway destinations you'd like to visit—and work from remotely if you decide to

- Photos of your loved ones as a reminder of what having a successful business can do for your family

- Cutouts of guilty pleasures (that fab pair of shoes, stunning piece of jewelry, new car)

- *et cetera*

Seeing it all laid out in a collage of words and pictures can motivate you to focus on what you need to bring your SMART Goals (Specific, Measurable, Achievable, Realistic, and Time-bound) within reach. It can inspire you, help you get unstuck, bring feelings of opportunity and passion, and connect your emotions to those goals. It can help you be confident even during the times when you just...*aren't*.

So what's your *why*? Have you still not written it out? Take a moment and do it now.

Right this very moment.

Now post it somewhere you can clearly see it.

You'll thank me later.

Note it...

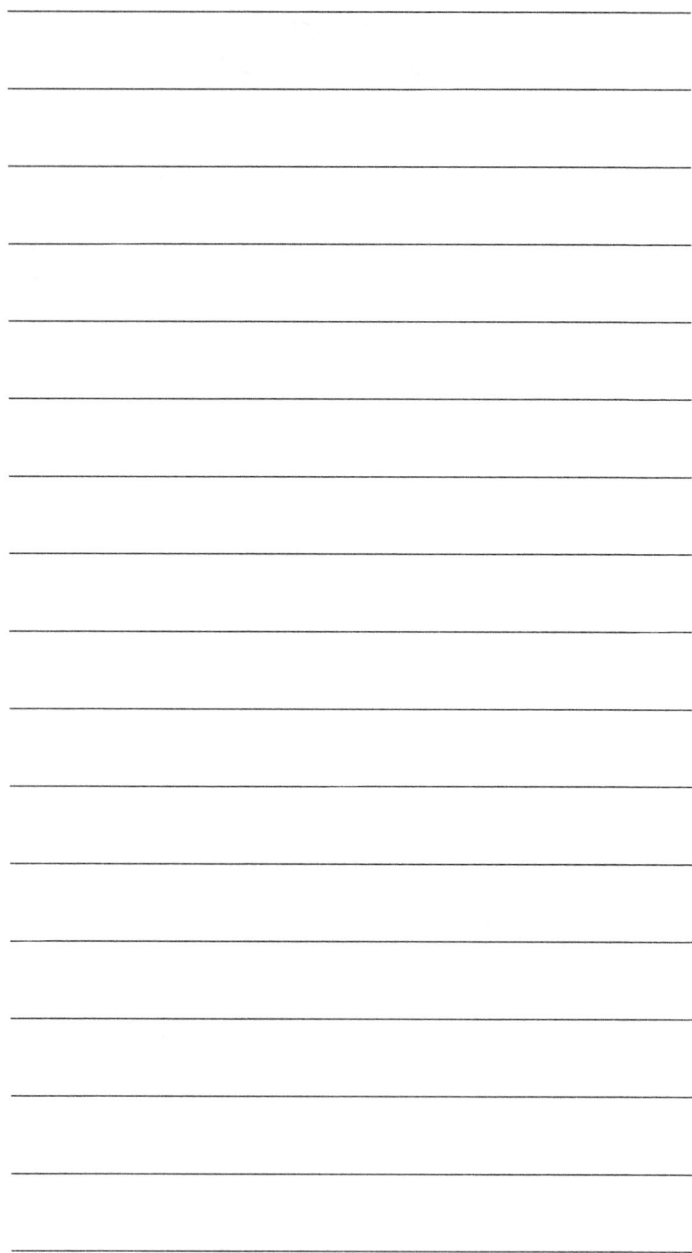

> Identify your ideal
> client as early on as
> possible in your
> business so that you
> can be intentional
> and strategic in your
> efforts to reach them.
>
> *Ask Cheri*

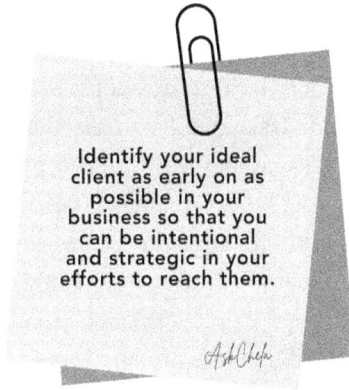

There's so much talk today about identifying and finding one's ideal client. It does, after all, help you clarify your business message and present it in such a way that it more easily reaches the consumers or clients who would be most interested in what you have to offer. That has always made sense to me. Why would I, after all, spend precious time and resources pursuing people who have zero need or interest in my services?

But when I first started my business in 2001, I had absolutely no idea who I considered to be my ideal client. Being in business for myself was, after all, completely new to me, and the virtual assistance industry was still in its infancy, so I didn't have anyone to advise me on how to land clients at all, let alone *ideal* clients. Who I preferred to work with wasn't really even a consideration. I just knew I needed an income. And I was willing to take on almost anyone.

And I did! I had a small list of occasional clients who

hired me to do the usual administrative stuff—mostly typing, stuffing envelopes, sending faxes, simple database-related activities, etc. And though my work was mostly remote, my clients were typically local to where I was living at the time, so there were some tasks that I was asked to do in-person or on-site (for events) as well.

As time went on, however, a much clearer picture of who I preferred to work with began to come into focus, as did a fuller acceptance that my clients and I could live states, even *countries* apart, and still get work done. Though I had a slow start in actually landing those preferred professionals, I began to explore ways that would put me in the same circles as them so that I could learn what they wanted and, even more importantly, determine how I could fulfill their specific needs with my services.

I knew I wanted to someday work with authors, and I began to wonder if it was possible for a Virtual Assistant to design a set of services that would appeal to these creatives. The idea made complete sense to me! I had, after all, written and self-published my first book a few years earlier (a young reader fiction book called *You're Too Much, Reggie Brown*, which I wrote under the pen name Kamichi Jackson), and I remember wishing I could just focus on writing and making appearances to share my book with my little audience of readers and not have to bother with the other details that came with my project. It occurred to me that other self-published or independently-published authors might feel the same.

So I did my research and discovered training that would allow me to offer a unique set of services that would be helpful to business owners writing books to establish themselves as experts in their respective fields. These professionals, I learned, were also often workshop facilitators, seminar presenters, keynote speakers, et cetera. They made their living with their words, and as a VA with both a strong Executive Assistant background and a firsthand—albeit *basic* at that time—understanding of the publishing industry, there were ways I could support them in getting those words out into the world.

Authors and speakers then became my ideal clients. Determining that and researching how I could be useful to them as a Virtual Author & Speaker Assistant completely changed my business going forward as I began to align myself not only with individual authors, but also with small and hybrid publishing companies that needed services like mine as they brought on more and more clients themselves.

Whether you offer general administrative services or have niched down to a very specific set of services, you should ask yourself the question *who is my ideal client?* at some point so that you have a better sense of how to direct your marketing efforts with the goal of landing that client. You are setting yourself up for failure if you don't determine that. You are losing precious time if you spend that time trying to reach out to anyone and everyone.

When you are clear on who you prefer to serve, your business messaging becomes concise, consistent, and appealing. Prospective clients will be drawn to you because you are speaking a language they understand, and they will feel more comfortable investing their hard-earned money into hiring you to help them in their business in a way that helps them grow it.

One of the exercises I take my coaching clients through is having them create an *avatar* of who that ideal client is for them. Some determine that they prefer to work with women, in some cases only with moms. Some prefer men, while others have no preference either way. Some want to work with startups, others want to work with more established businesses. An industry-specific client base is preferred by some (i.e. fashion, fitness, wellness, event planning, technology, pet care). Some restrict their client lists to the same time zone, others to a different time zone that fits their schedule better. You get the point—that *when you know who your ideal client is, then your messaging and marketing become more meaningful, and that comes across in your interactions with business owners anxious to hire someone who can take ownership of the tasks that prevent them from focusing on growing their business.*

So take a moment and go through the exercise of actually identifying and making note of who you consider to be your ideal client. Make a list you can add to or revise as you get a clearer view of who those professionals are. Need a more visual idea? Go through magazines and cut out pictures of what your ideal client looks like (a marketing exec in a suit, a parent working from home, an artist creating a masterpiece, a small team of t-shirt and baseball cap-wearing entrepreneurs huddled together around a bunch of monitors in the office, et cetera). Including these images in your ideal client notes will help you begin to hone in on the work they do that may require your services.

Once you've gone through the steps, do yourself a favor and write it out as in this sample below (and post it where you can see it):

IDEAL CLIENT STATEMENT
AskChela works with business owners who want to publish books as a way to expand their brands and establish themselves as experts in their fields.

Take the time to go through this exercise. It's key to your business development efforts, it will help you pitch to potential clients with confidence, and it will make a huge difference in your business success overall.

Note it...

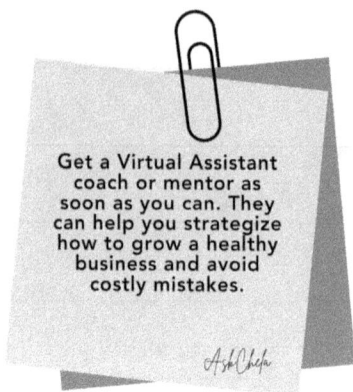

In 2023, I was a guest on longtime Virtual Assistant Coach and Mentor Katie Tew's "Up Close & Virtual" podcast, and Katie posed a question I couldn't wait to answer: *how important did I think it was for a VA to have a coach and/or mentor?*

As I wrote in the opening of this book, the industry was not in place at the time I was getting started, so there were a lot of things I had to figure out on my own for the first few years. Sometimes I made good business moves, other times I did not. It would've been so much easier—not to mention more financially sound—to have had someone guide me through the maze of what was an almost completely unknown way of working back then.

These days, as Katie and I discussed, the industry has come so much further, and there is an abundance of information available to people interested in starting a VA career. Courses, webinars, blogs, videos, downloadable this and that, et cetera. The internet is simply *teeming* with advice on the topic. So much so, in fact, that overwhelm can easily set in, and a person can quickly find themselves stuck in a place where they are unable to move beyond the research phase to actually getting started.

This is where a coach or mentor can help. This person can help you wade through, or even bypass, the sea of you-too-can-start-a-Virtual-Assistant-business information out there. They can help you talk through the specific details of what you want your VA business to look like *for you*—and then empower you with the roadmap to help you reach the goal. Most importantly, they can help you avoid bad business decisions that cause you to spend precious time, money, and resources unnecessarily.

Having said that, the best type of coach or mentor to hire is *someone who has actual experience as a VA*. Someone who has worked in the trenches and who has been exposed to the unique struggles of starting and running a VA business is able to speak from a place of authenticity and empathy. They are able to help you stay in the proper mindset to work past the challenges and keep going in your business. These are qualities you will appreciate deeply as you travel your own journey.

Make sure you work with a coach or mentor *who emphasizes the need for consistent business development*. Clients aren't likely to come falling at your feet and begging to work with you! A coach or mentor can help you come up with and implement traditional and creative ways to get on and stay on the radar of potential clients who may hire you in the future as their businesses grow.

What else to look for in a coach or mentor? A *connection*. Something about the person that resonates with you personally. Perhaps they are a mom with a family situation similar to yours, or they are a caregiver to an aging parent, and you can relate to that. Perhaps you both come from the same cultural background, and that makes you comfortable. Maybe their compelling story about escaping Corporate America makes you cheer. Or their dissatisfaction with working a low-paying retail job is all too familiar to you.

Whatever the reason, find that connection. It will help you develop a more meaningful professional relationship with that person, which will empower you to reach your business goals more quickly and progressively.

Communication style is also extremely important, would you not agree? Think about the way you best relate to people in other areas of your life. Are you a shy person who is more comfortable interacting with people who are kind and nurturing? Are you someone who speaks bluntly and prefers to deal with similar no-nonsense personalities? Only you can decide what works for you. It comes down to whatever will make their business advice most acceptable and palatable to you.

But what if you can't afford to engage a coach or mentor at all right now? My best advice: *get yourself in the mindset of having one until you are in a financial position to actually do so.* What does that look like? Here are some ways:

- Find one or two VA experts whose message or compelling story resonates with you personally. They tend to be very generous with their knowledge, so follow their social media channels, read their blogs, download their freebies, watch their videos, register for their low-cost webinars, et cetera. In every case, take helpful notes and implement the strategies you learn. You're essentially engaging them as your coach or mentor, at little or no cost to you!

- Join Facebook, Alignable, or LinkedIn groups that have been created specifically for VAs. There are some really amazing ones out there. Do a search, if you haven't already done so. Join, engage, and allow yourself to be coached and mentored by other VAs in this way.

Last note: a Virtual Assistant coach or mentor can be helpful at any point in your business journey, not just when you're getting started. Keep that in mind—and be sure to avail yourself of their expertise whenever you feel the need for a bit of guidance to move you forward.

Note it...

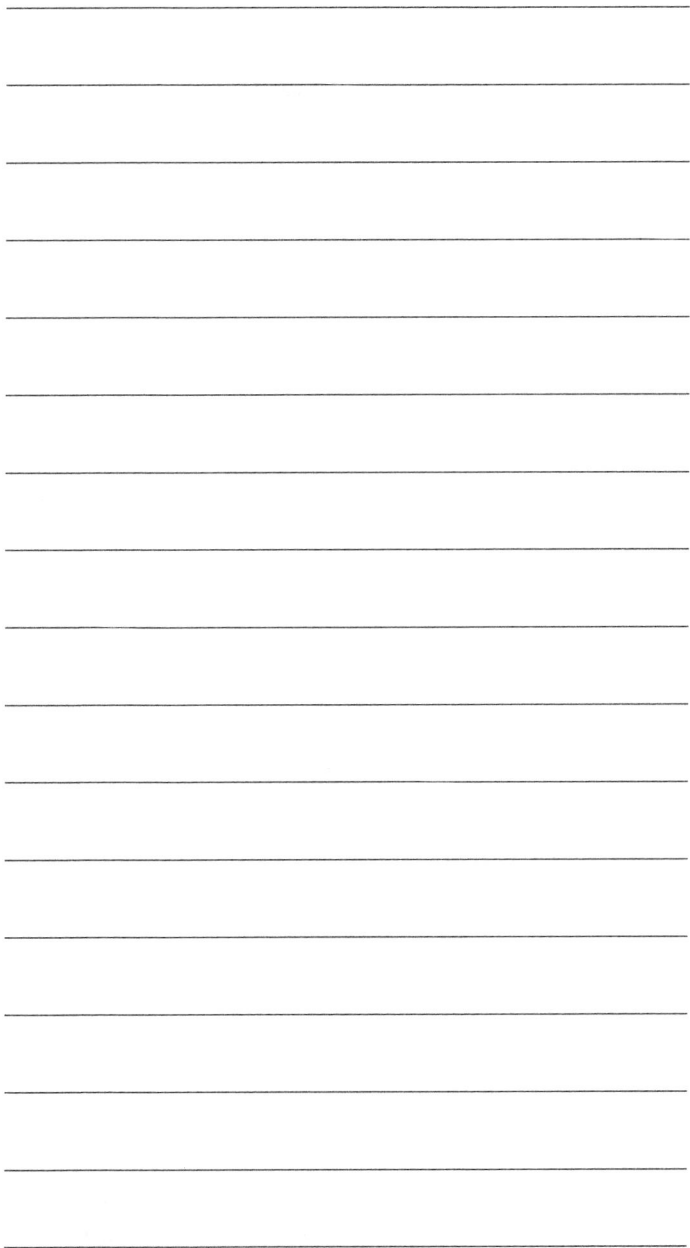

> **Create and implement a consistent business development routine as early as possible. If you haven't done so yet, start right now.**
>
> *AshChafa*

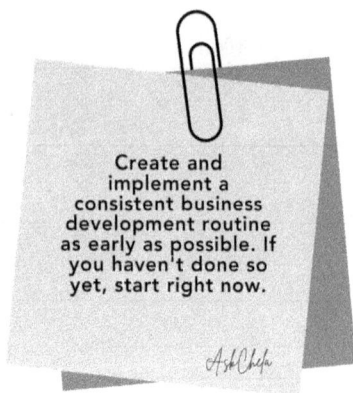

When I first started my business back in 2001, I did so with no plan—just an abstract idea of the administrative services I wanted to offer and a vague sense of the types of companies that might be interested in hiring me to deliver them. I knew nothing of business development. I'd heard the term before, of course, but only in the context of Corporate America. Thinking back, I suppose I knew that midsize companies also had entire business development departments, and that small companies at least had an employee in that role. But I don't think I fully understood and appreciated what that would look like for me within my own one-woman operation.

I remember researching potential clients, and I remember doing outreach (sometimes via email and sometimes via physical mailing out of marketing materials I'd created) that would lead to the occasional follow-up from someone I'd contacted. I would get clients from time to time—so in my own way, I was going through some of the motions of business development. But it was haphazard and inconsistent, and it didn't result in nearly enough new business to keep my practice afloat on a full-time basis in the beginning.

I fully understand now the need to get in business development mode from the very start—and to stay in that mode even if you have a full roster of clients. You never know what challenges and lulls are on the horizon, after all, whether within a specific industry, or as the result of some unexpected worldwide event that affects the economy at large. The reality is that you could lose one or more (or even *all*) of your clients and suddenly find yourself in panic-mode trying to replace that income.

I don't like that mode, LOL. So in the past few years, I have put together a simple business development binder for myself that makes it easier for me to go about this necessary function in a consistent, organized, and even *fun* way. When I follow this regimen, I feel comfortable and confident as I go about running my business. When I don't, I fall back into those moments of panic, because I know firsthand how quickly things can change from good to bad to worse in a short period of time.

I'm not saying this to scare you—but I am saying it to impress upon you the importance of getting this part of your entrepreneurial journey in place sooner rather than later.

So let's back up for a moment and really nail down a high-level view of what business development is: *literally the practice of developing new business*:

- identifying and pursuing new opportunities

- maximizing the value of the clients you already have

- building and nurturing strategic relationships with key connections and referral partners in order to gain new clients

Within each element of this formula, of course, are sub-elements. I won't go into them here—it's a big topic that could fill an entire book on its own. The good news is that you can find lots of information online to get you started. My recommendation would be to do your homework to first discover what business development looks like for a solopreneur in general, then a Virtual Assistant specifically—and then adopt the techniques that fit:

- your business

- your specific needs

- your unique personality

- your personal level of comfort

When I was putting together my personal weekly strategy, I created a bullet point list of the things I was doing that had either already successfully resulted in landing a new client, or that I could see had the potential to do so with a little tweaking. Then I broke that list down into a sub-bulleted list with more details. That initial list and all its updated versions eventually became the eight-part framework for a weekly plan I enjoy following.

And here's a side note: the tasks I identify as actual client-attracting ones don't come until the end of the process, the eighth and final component of my framework. It makes sense: if I am consistently doing the first seven things on my plan, then the last thing—actually marketing and pitching my services to potential clients—makes attracting those professionals organically much easier.

There are no hard and fast rules, but this process works for me. Who knows? It could work for you too. You might even come to love it the way I do—especially as you see your efforts paying off in the way of new or consistent business.

And if your research and planning just becomes too overwhelming, you can always visit my website to learn more about the AskChela BizDev Binder for Virtual Assistants. It'll save you lots of time and effort by empowering you to begin building your own awesome binder and attracting your ideal clients more quickly.

Note it...

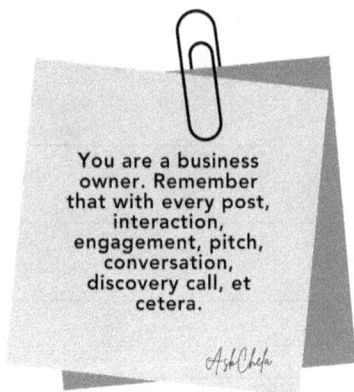

Imagine you are in the market for a new livingroom set. You likely do some research from home, check your finances, decide on your budget. This is a big purchase, an important investment, and you need to be sure it's a proper fit. Beyond being useful and functional, you hope that this new addition to the space in your home will be a long-term one as well. Making an educated, informed decision is a must.

You head out to the "furniture district" and you're immediately overwhelmed by the number of stores that line the streets. Several vendors are selling the same pieces and promising the same result—that you'll be happiest with your purchase if you buy from *them*. Their prices are competitive and within your budget, so your choices aren't narrowed down any based on affordability alone. This decision is harder than you thought it would be.

What if, though, several of these vendors start waving their arms about, making long-winded and loud pitches from within the doorways of their stores, attempting to get your attention and flag you down so you'll step over to them and allow them to tell you in more detail why you should shop their store over another one? What if they start telling you how much they really need you to buy from them—they have kids at home who they're having trouble feeding? The rent or mortgage is due. They've been at this business for a while now, and nothing is working out no matter how hard they try. If you buy from them, they say in so many words, it will change *everything*, and they are even willing to give you a deep discount just so you'll go with them over someone else.

Would this tug at your heartstrings make you inclined to spend with this person the limited time you have available to explore your options? Or does it bother you a bit that they used this particular approach to pitch their wares to you? Maybe they do have the best product. Maybe they don't. The reality is that it's simply an unknown at this time. That's the nature of doing business.

As Virtual Assistants, if we're not careful, we can easily and quite unfortunately come across this same way. How many times, for instance, have you seen this happen in a VA Facebook group: a small business owner, perhaps already unsure of how to go about hiring and engaging a VA, posts a #JOBOPP and is immediately inundated with responses. Many pitches are professional and meet the requirements of the poster, but others are *literally* desperate cries for attention meant to tug at the heartstrings in an emotional effort to sway the person towards hiring them. They have children who need to be fed, are facing being unhoused because the rent or mort-gage is past due. They may not only post this publicly—some VAs will even go so far as to send a direct message or email to the poster to ensure that their pleas are seen.

This is a lesson I'm sharing as someone who has been on the receiving end of these emails and messages. *Please understand that I'm not including this to shame anyone who has ever done this*. I, like so many in this industry, have felt that level of desperation before, especially in the early days. But it's important to keep it to yourself in your public posts and interactions. The reality is that business owners don't typically want to be approached that way. *You* as a business owner yourself likely don't want to be approached that way. It's not appealing, and it likely won't do anything more than annoy the poster. This is, after all, an investment for them. It's a necessary one, they've decided, having done enough research to know that adding a VA to their team can help them grow and scale their business. They know how important it is to choose the right person. Whether or not the relationship will work out remains to be seen, but they expect a professional experience in the process from the very start.

It is certainly understandable that we all need to vent from time to time, and our online connections may be the only place we can do so—among people who can feel our pain and understand our plight. We may not have a support system at home or in our friendship circles. Even more sadly, some VAs may even have people close to them who are just waiting for them to fail in this venture.

A VA may feel the weight of that when they come online to make connections, and in most cases, they are looking for social interactions that will make them feel lighter and hopeful.

I remember once seeing a VA post that very comment in a popular Facebook group. She expressed that she had come into the group that morning for encouragement, because no one in her personal circle believed in her. Instead, she wrote, she had scrolled through more negative threads than positive ones, and it had left her more discouraged than ever.

I was so deeply touched by her post and its sheer honesty.

But what literally made my eyes well up with tears (I can be emotional sometimes) is how hundreds of VAs in the group responded to her with comments expressing their own vulner-abilities—along with words of hope and well wishes that surely carried her through those dark moments.

This is, once again, where our community shines at its brightest! In our crowd, you can find a listening ear, a supportive virtual shoulder to cry on, and most importantly, sage advice to help you move beyond emotions and into a mindset that can help you strategize with a clearer head. Avail yourself of these relationships. And remember to give more emotionally than you take. Lifting up others can lift you up as well and help you keep going.

So here's the key takeaway: as a general note of best prac-tice, venting in an open forum such as a public Facebook group (where there are potentially hundreds of other entrepre-neurs looking to engage VA services for their businesses) is not recommended. Explore alternative ways to express frus-trations and disappointments in private—but continue to put your best professional selves forward in public. That's how you attract clients and grow your VA business.

Note it...

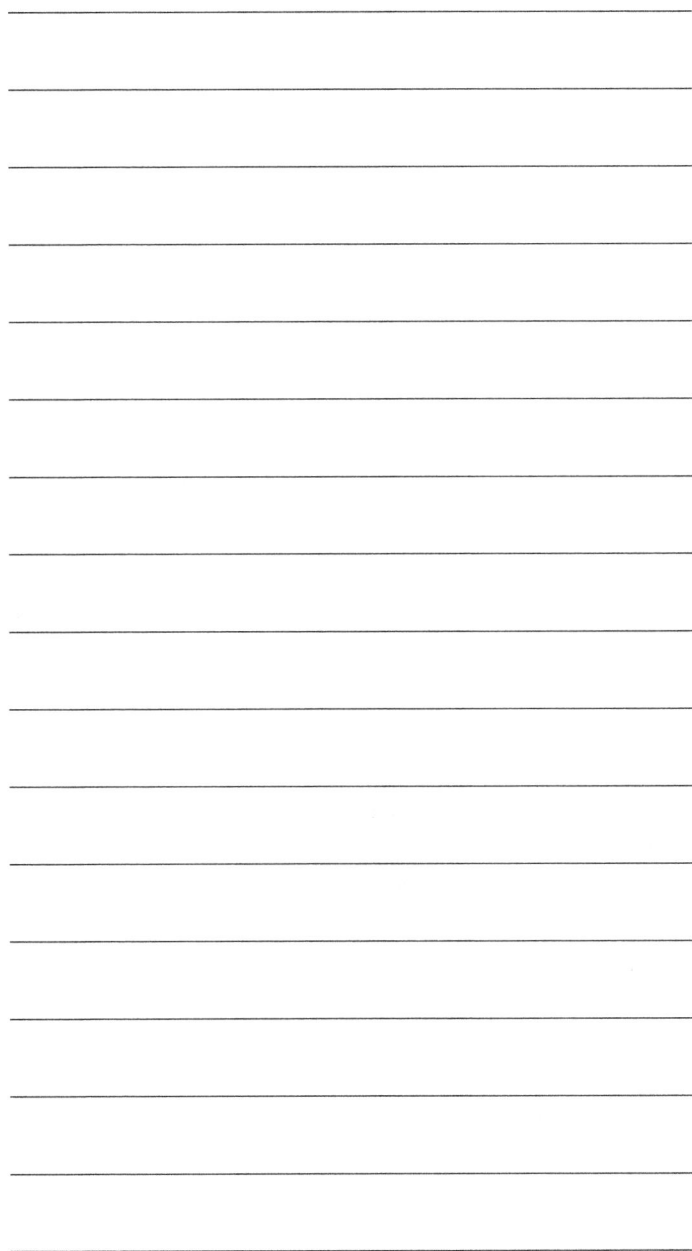

Make good
communication a
priority in your
business to attract
potential clients and
maintain strong
relationships with
current ones.

Ask Chefa

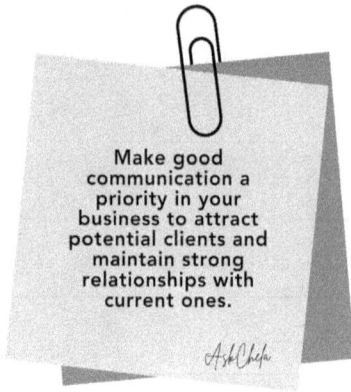

I grew up across from a small library that I visited several times a week from the moment I was allowed to cross the quiet street by myself. I spent hours there in the children's section on the first floor of the building, poring over short books I could read on the spot, then loading up and leaving with my arms full of longer books I could dive into at home in the days to follow. I eventually graduated to titles for older readers—on the second and third stories of the building, and I devoured those quickly too. Once I was old enough to drive, I was able to make frequent visits to the main library down-town in our city, and I could be found camping out there for hours on end.

I was obviously an avid reader. What I didn't know back then was that my appetite for well-chosen words on a page was also strengthening my communication skills, which empowered me to do well in school, most especially in Language Arts and English classes. I loved writing, and I remember receiving high grades on book reports and other such assignments. I didn't aspire to be a writer or a published author back then. I had no idea that I even had the ability to write anything more than a few homework pages. I just knew I loved words and the power they held, though I didn't fully appreciate how that love would play into my future work life.

This early look at communication helped me land my first summer office job at age fifteen. It exposed me to other amazing on-the-job learning opportunities once I graduated high school and started full-time in the workforce. And it has served me well in my journey from administrative employee to administrative business owner.

Which is why I work so hard to properly communicate what it is that AskChela does—with every word on my social media accounts, websites, and printed marketing materials. In my pitches, discovery calls, and podcast interviews. I think and rethink everything I communicate verbally, non-verbally, and in writing, because it affects my business and brand.

Like it or not, we are almost always immediately judged by the way we communicate. Our facial expressions and body language—both of which are on full display in our networking and online interactions with potential clients—can determine whether we successfully land the client or not.

Our written communications can obviously do the same. The reality is that, no matter how advanced we are in our skill set, a lack of proper and timely communication can frustrate a client, who is investing hard-earned funds in us with the expectation that doing so will leave them with the time and clarity to focus on matters that will help them continue to build the business.

How do you feel you're doing in this area? Is your communication style client-attracting? Or do you think this is an area in your business that could use some improvement?

It's definitely worth the effort to level up your communication skills! Not only does it have the potential to help you land new clients—it can also increase your value in their eyes. When clients understand and appreciate what you bring to their business, they typically expect that engaging your services will involve a bigger investment on their part, especially if those services will involve you communicating with their end clients on their behalf. At the end of the day, that translates to more income for you.

So what are practical ways you can commit to making better communication a bigger part of your VA business—whether in your marketing efforts, outreach, or client interactions? Here are a few basic but important suggestions:

- *Be very careful about your spelling, grammar, punctuation, and sentence structure.* Most software programs will flag on screen any instances where edits can or should be made to improve the understanding of any words or thoughts you've typed. There are also several browser add-ons that can be installed to accomplish this and more. Pay attention to these closely. While it's true that they aren't always 100% correct, they are a good start to improving your message.

- *Create simple template language* for outreach, common email replies, responses to your website contact form, pitch and discovery call prep, et cetera. Doing so will make your life easier, help you feel better prepared for these interactions, and give you the kind of confidence that is attractive to prospective clients, referral partners, and others in your professional circle. Side note: don't just cut and paste into these templates. Take a few minutes to customize the language enough that it feels personal to the receiver, especially if you hope to be in business with them.

- *Be smart about the way you communicate on Facebook and any other social media accounts* you use. Colleagues looking to make referrals, not to mention other business owners looking to hire, could be watching (to be on the safe side and to keep yourself in check, just assume they are). The way you communicate online can work either *against* or *for* you. Be sure it's the latter.

- *Review your website content regularly* (perhaps on your monthly CEO Day) for dead links, typos, misinformation, images that don't load properly, et cetera. You want your online home to communicate that you care about the visitor experience, which will hopefully lead a prospective client to engage your services or share your site with their colleagues.

In my opinion, however, good communication is even more important once you are actually providing services to the client. At this point, it becomes more about relationship management, which is key to a long-term working arrangement and, ultimately, longevity in your VA career.

What does this relationship management communication style look like? In some ways, it's similar to the way an administrative employee would engage with their Executive:

- Acknowledging receipt of emails—with either a reply that provides the information requested or confirming that it will be provided ASAP or by a specific time/date.

- Is there a change to the delivery timeline of a project? Update the client with clear details that will allow them to make whatever adjustments they need to on their end.

- Planning to be away from your desk for several days? You typically don't need to explain why, but it's common courtesy to let your clients know that you may be unreachable. And it's absolutely imperative to do so if you must cancel a scheduled meeting with them, or they are expecting to be able to reach you to move a time-sensitive project forward.

It's very much worth interjecting here the thought that there needs to be a careful balance to your communication with your client. You are as much a business owner as they are, meaning that *you are your own boss*. Communicate in a way that sets boundaries for each of you, incorporating a high level of professionalism combined with candor, honesty, and clarity. It will make for a much better working relationship with fewer misunderstandings and/or errors.

Note it...

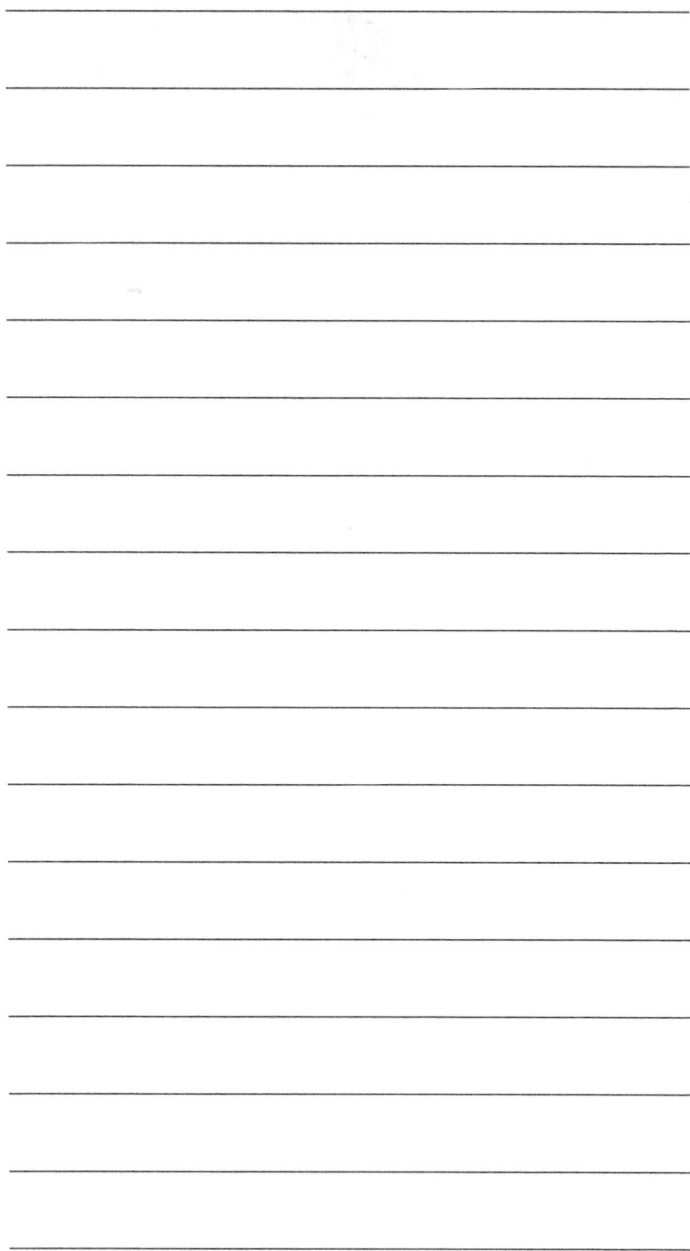

> Put your unique personality into your business. You'll have more fun with it, which will take you through the hard times. And it'll reflect in how you engage professionally, which attracts clients.
>
> *Ask Chefe*

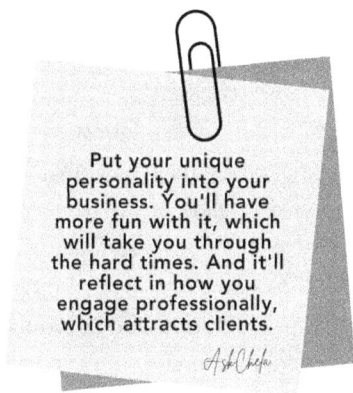

Have you ever heard of Marie Forleo? She's an incredibly successful entrepreneur with tens of millions of fans and followers, a highly successful podcast, a widely-watched television show, a New York Times bestselling book...and so many more accomplishments, including being named by Oprah as a thought leader for the next generation.

But before Marie became all these things, she was a hip hop-loving MTV-choreographing fitness enthusiast. One can only imagine how many well-meaning advisors, friends, and family members likely told her to leave that side of her out of her new business venture if she wanted to be taken seriously. She didn't do that, you'll see if you watch her earlier videos on YouTube where—right in the middle of sage business advice—the camera suddenly cuts to her and a couple of backup dancers in choreographed steps to popular hip-hop songs. Rather than abandon a side of her that is so much a part of her, she dug in, embedding it deeply into her brand, even bringing it to her 2019 *Everything is Figureoutable* book launch party extravaganza. Her willingness to market herself in such an unconventional way surely made her stand out among hundreds, even thousands, of entrepreneurs doling out business advice to similar audiences.

I've learned something from following Marie and others like her: clients and colleagues will always get to see the professional, buttoned-up side of my personality in our inter-actions—but it's also okay for me to be a little goofy and show a bit of the *silly* side of my personality in certain situa-tions. Like when I'm mentoring and coaching other VAs, for instance. It's okay to post and comment publicly on things that make me giggle (I really, really love to laugh). It's okay to admit that I watch Disney and Nickelodeon shows, even now that my nieces and nephew are older and outgrew those channels long, long ago. It's okay to talk proudly about my need for daily naps—and how they are not just for toddlers or the elderly anymore. And it's okay to incorporate my love for old-school R&B by singing a few snippets on TikTok or IG simply because I want to.

These are the things that put my personality on full display, letting potential clients see that I am a fun and friendly person who (usually) has work-life balance and a positive mindset. This draws them to me and makes me and my business stand out. In a discovery call with me, they can feel my passion for my business because it's reflected in how I run it and how I talk to others about what I do. They know I'll bring that same passion to any work we do together.

And here's a truth: if for some reason my personality is *unappealing* to someone, that's okay too. It only means we are just not a match for each other, and we're able to avoid losing precious time finding that out. In the short and long run, that's best for all involved.

It's your turn. What is it about you that makes you stand out? Are you:

...a strong communicator?
This trait is valued by clients and should be a priority in your business.

...self-motivated?
Clients want to hire VAs who will confirm that they understand the assignment, push through any challenges that arise, and keep things moving forward.

...a leader?
In general, this is just a great trait to have, even if you are a business owner who has no team to lead.

...a visionary?
The ability to have a clear vision of what a client needs and think through the related opportunities is appealing on so many levels.

...a decision-maker?
What client wouldn't appreciate a VA who can quickly assess a situation and make appropriate decisions to move it forward?

It isn't always easy to identify within ourselves the traits that make us shine, but as you can see, it's important to do so. Take a look at the short checklist below to see if any of these describe you:

Active Listener	Adaptable	Adventurous
Ambitious	Calm	Collaborative
Compassionate	Confident	Creative
Curious	Dependable	Disciplined
Empathetic	Ethical	Flexible
Honest	Open-Minded	Optimistic
Persistent	Problem-Solver	Punctual
Resilient	Resourceful	Self-Aware

How did you do? Were you able to identify any of these traits in yourself? Did others come to mind? Do you feel able to put these aspects of your personality on display as part of your business brand in some way?

The lesson is this: don't be afraid to let people see who you truly are. Your unique personality can be one of the most effective ways to stand out and make a lasting impression. It also adds a *human touch* to what you do (take *that*, AI). If you let it, your personality could be one of your best client attraction methods ever!

Note it...

Try to do work that truly excites you and makes you look forward to sitting down at your desk each day. That's the joy of being in business for yourself!

Ask Chefa

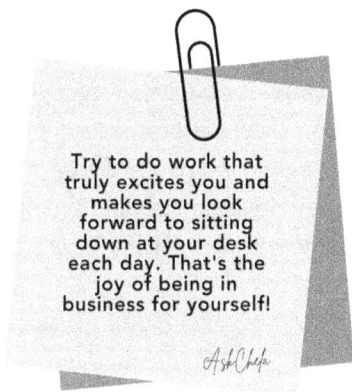

As I wrote a few pages ago, I grew up across from a small library where I spent hours and hours on end each week reading every book I could get my hands on. My passion for books only grew over the years, and I decided early on that I wanted to work in the publishing industry. The big New York publishing houses were only a quick train ride away, and as I moved through my public school years, I kept this as a goal. I firmly believed that having a strong administrative skill set would always serve me well, no matter where life took me, and I figured it would be the easiest way to get my foot in the door and then move around from there.

Life didn't take me down that road, but my desire to work in publishing never diminished. *Self*-publishing was becoming a more acceptable option for many writers who weren't getting traditional book deals, and it was happening around the very same time I was discovering that I had stories of my own to tell. As I began to learn more about the industry, I decided to dive in using myself as a way to learn more about this aspect of publishing.

I will never forget the pure joy I felt when I was writing my first book. *You're Too Much, Reggie Brown*, which I've since come to appreciate was before its time in its genre, was about a nine-year-old book-loving African American girl who often found herself in head-shaking situations that always resulted in sweet, teachable moments young readers and their parents came to love.

What was even more exciting to me than writing *Reggie Brown* was promoting it! Getting out there, making classroom and book festival appearances, doing live readings, signing books—all of it brought a sense of satisfaction I can barely describe in words. Having eager readers lined up with my book clutched to their chests waiting to meet me? I hold those memories close and smile at them even now.

Over time, seeds were being planted in unexpected ways to bring to fruition the dream I'd always had of working in publishing, being immersed in manuscripts, and surrounded by bound books containing stories—both real and imagined —written by people who were brave and creative enough to share them. Only this dream was better, because it also brought in another important part of my journey: virtual assistance.

I wish I could say that everything then fell into place at that time.

It didn't.

And it would be some time before it did.

Yes, the VA industry was taking shape and form and becoming more acceptable to savvy entrepreneurs who under-stood how it would have a positive impact on their business model. But it wasn't happening soon enough for me, and my new ideal clients weren't coming as quickly as I had hoped.

That's not unusual, of course. Most VAs will tell you that the hardest part of getting their businesses off the ground after they've launched is actually landing paying clients—ideal or otherwise. Weeks, even months, may go by before they get a discovery call on their calendar. Desperate and panicky, they typically take on whoever is willing to hire them. There may be red flags everywhere, flying high and bright, but they may choose to ignore them because they need the work.

I'm guilty of having done that too. Even in more recent years, when a challenging economy or a chronic health issue has affected my client roster. Worry sets in, and I find myself taking on a project I wouldn't typically take on, even though I know early in the discovery call that it won't bring me the joy factor I look for when choosing work. It isn't long, of course, before I wish I'd turned it down and am literally counting the days to when it'll be over so I can get back to only doing the work I love.

I don't like being in that mental space, feeling those feelings. I went into business for myself, after all, so that I could wake up every morning excited to sit down at my desk and start my day. Or, worst case scenario, at least not *hate* what I have on my to-do list for the day. It dredges up memories of working in Corporate America, when I knew everyday would be the same as the one before: answering phones, taking and relaying messages, coordinating meetings on multiple calendars, researching and booking travel requests…*ugh.* The very thought of it brings on a numbness I can't put into words. Wait…the phrase *soul-sucking* comes to mind. And one thing I know for sure is that I don't like feeling that way in my business, when I have full control over the work I literally *choose* to do.

Which is why I try so hard to now only do the work that excites me—working with authors and speakers helping them hands-on with tasks directly related to the publishing of their work. Not their calendaring, not booking their travel, not handling their personal tasks, but, rather, managing their publishing projects and helping them brainstorm ways to market, promote, and repurpose their content. That's where I sparkle and shine. That's what gives me calm and a sense of purpose. *Ahhhh*….

I want that for you too. I understand, yes, that you may be in the beginning stages of your virtual assistant business, or perhaps you've been at this for a while and circumstances have shifted and you find yourself panicky about landing your next client. I know that feeling. But unless you're content with taking on anyone and everyone that comes your way, I want you to do this:

- Figure out what really makes you want to sit down at your desk everyday and feel like you're doing exactly what you were built to do…or at least gives you a measure of peace while doing it

- Nail down who your ideal client is, the work they do, the services they'll need from you, et cetera, so that you're only pursuing opportunities that meet your *wants* (or at least limit you from taking on work you don't enjoy)

- If you do find yourself constantly taking on work you don't enjoy, *explore why that is*—then take definite steps toward adjusting your mindset so that you begin to attract the work you want to do

In my opinion, it comes down to this: *what's the point of being in business for yourself if you can't do something you like?* Especially if you willingly left a somewhat stable situation to work on your own. Why not design a business that not only gives you the income you need, but also satisfies you on a deeper level?

I'm here to help you get there.

Note it...

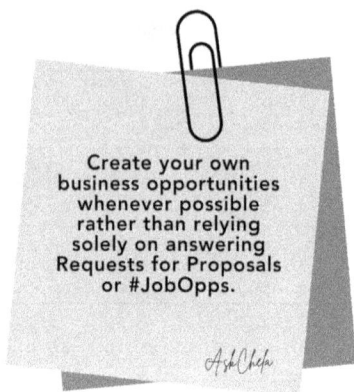

Create your own
business opportunities
whenever possible
rather than relying
solely on answering
Requests for Proposals
or #JobOpps.

Ask Chiefa

Over the course of my career as a Virtual Assistant, I have only ever replied to three or four Requests for Proposals. And if my memory serves me correctly, not a single one resulted in a request for additional information, let alone a discovery call. Perhaps my pricing was off, or my language was not descriptive enough. Or maybe there were dozens and dozens of other applicants, and my proposal was never even seen! Whatever the reason, answering RFPs and bidding for gigs didn't work for me, which was why I eventually decided to seek out and/or create my own opportunities.

Some of the most successful people in the world will tell you that there came a time in their lives—whether earlier or later in their careers—when they realized that waiting around for opportunities to come to them just wasn't going to get them anywhere in the journey they'd chosen for themselves. For reasons known and/or unknown, their talent continued to go unnoticed, even as others around them, some with comparable abilities (some even with less), experienced levels of success they could only dream of. Like talented actors who are considered "not the Hollywood type" and decide to write, fund, produce and star in their own productions. Or amazingly talented musicians who produce albums independently because record labels aren't willing to take a chance on them. And writers who don't get the attention they want from traditional publishing houses, so they create their own publishing companies and self-publish their work.

Deciding to make their own way in their respective field was the best decision they could ever have made, these people will often tell their fans. Creating their own opportunities made the difference and jumpstarted their careers, setting them down a path of success that also positioned them to take and keep more control of their next moves.

Shortly after niching down to providing services to authors and speakers, I decided to try creating an opportunity where there didn't appear to be one. I was attending a small business webinar series by Office Depot, and it was being hosted by a woman who I quickly decided I wanted to work with. She was an accomplished author and speaker, and I liked her business message. I sent her either a chat or an email—I don't recall anymore. Surprisingly, she responded, which resulted in a discovery call that led to her becoming one of my first author/speaker clients. Her business focus completely shifted after a few years, so she is no longer in need of my unique skill set. But we remain in touch, and over the years, she has referred a few ideal clients to me.

If I had waited around for her to post an RFP somewhere, my response to it might've gotten swept up in a mountain of other responses from qualified VAs. In fact, if I had waited to see if she even needed help at all, she and I may never have connected. I just knew that I wanted to work with her, and I figured why not reach out to see if she happened to need another team member at that time. She did. I gained a new client quite unexpectedly.

So now I teach my coachees, mentees, and workshop attendees to make creating their own opportunities a big part of their business development plan. Not that I discourage maintaining an active profile on freelancer sites like Upwork, Fiverr, or other such online spaces. Why not utilize these platforms? Doing so can indeed lead to new or unexpected business.

But my recommendation is to not just rely on those outlets. Find your own opportunities as well. Considering the number of small businesses around the world (with more and more popping up every year), your client pool is vast, even after you narrow it down to who you've determined is your *ideal* client.

How do you learn what business moves they are making and determine how they might need your help if only they knew your VA practice existed? By making it a habit to read and watch business news, whether it's local to you or across the country (maybe even the globe). What does that look like?

Let's say you're scrolling through one of the news sites and you come across a story that a company out in Phoenix, Arizona is opening a satellite office in your state, maybe even your city. That company will almost certainly assemble and send a small team of their employees to help prepare for the opening of that office. And they will almost certainly need someone in an administrative capacity to oversee and take care of certain tasks that are best done on-site and in-person. It may be too early in their plans to relocate one of their current admins for this new location, and it might not make sense just yet to engage a local employment or temp agency to hire someone locally full-time...*see where I am going with this?*

What they might consider—if approached in the right way with the right pitch—is engaging the services of a Virtual Assistant who is already working from their own home office and who is available for the interim on a scaled-down schedule until they are ready to make more permanent arrangements.

A VA who has made it a habit to read the business pages and comes across an item like this could see this as an opportunity for a new client. A little research into the company's products or services, the story behind the decision to move to the area, how their presence plays into the local business community—all these factors and more become the basis for a strong letter of introduction that could result in a discovery call that leads to a solid new client relationship.

All as the result of a few daily minutes of scrolling through business news websites.

True—scenarios like this one may not happen as often as we'd like. But this will hopefully plant the idea in your head to always *be in the mindset that you can create your own opportunities* if you stay on the lookout for them.

Closer to home, of course, is a much easier way to make unexpected business connections. Which is why consistent networking with other business owners, within our industry as well as outside of it, is key to landing clients for your VA practice. It's not as difficult to do as you might think, though it definitely involves a bit of strategy—and a healthy dose of courage (which you likely have at least a bit of, since you've chosen to step out into the world as an entrepreneur).

By *strategy* I mean sitting down and drafting at least some sort of plan as to how and where you will meet potential clients and/or referral partners. What questions you'll ask to break the ice and learn more about their business. Which services you offer that you feel could address the pain points of their business, and just the right pitch to make to convince them to engage those services.

By *courage* I mean stepping away from the safety and comfort of your workspace and joining local networking groups in person, shaking hands, exchanging business cards (I still believe in the power of a good business card), all with people you likely don't know at first. Or if you're homebound like me, putting on a pretty blouse or a crisp shirt, turning on the camera, getting my lighting just right, and networking virtually with a group of other business owners over Zoom, Google Meet, or some other such platform.

Whatever your networking method, the goal is to create your own opportunities as often as you can so that you are in control. Put on your thinking cap and find creative ways to get the attention of your ideal client. You can do this!

Note it...

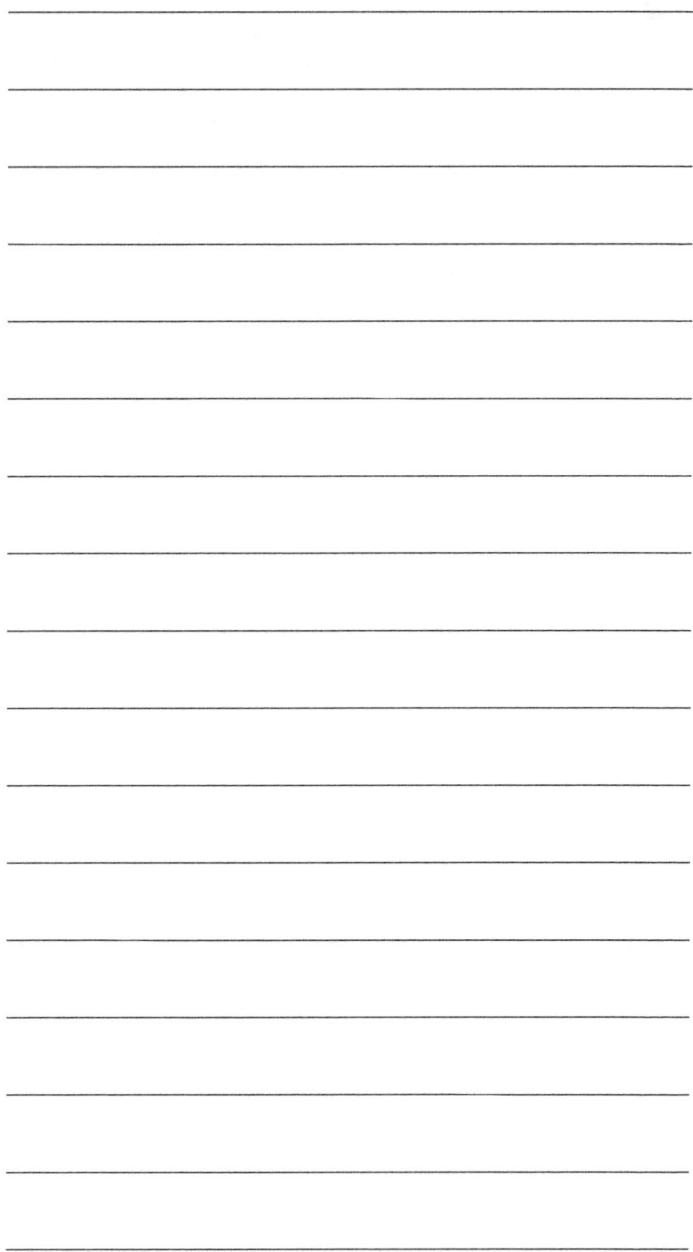

Don't get stuck in the planning phase of any aspect of your business. Take decisive action and make moves to implement your ideas.

Ash Chelsa

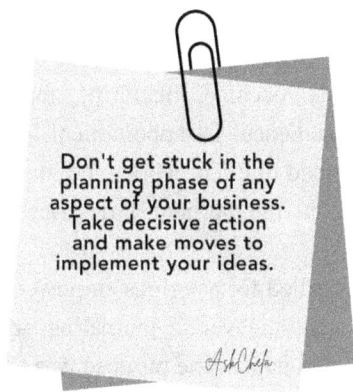

Honestly, I feel like a complete hypocrite on this one. But since I am being transparent…

I overthink things when it comes to my own processes and projects (for some reason, this doesn't happen when I am working on client projects). The perfectionist in me just won't let things go sometimes, and I find myself planning, planning, planning…then delaying, delaying…and *delaying* some more until I've blown up the timeline I created for myself. It's absolutely frustrating. And it can easily lead me to a negative headspace.

In fact, I decided over the pandemic that I wanted to "refresh" my business. I wanted to do more coaching and mentoring because I love our industry so much, and I want everyone else to see how amazing it is. I know firsthand how working in my business addressed my financial needs in the midst of several chronic health issues, and I wanted others in similar circumstances to see how being a VA might just help them too.

Ask me how far I got with that dream over the pandemic. Not very, I'll tell you. I had lots of client work, which was great. But I didn't make much progress at all with the plans I had for getting my coaching, mentoring, and content services out to a wider audience. Disappointment in myself—not to mention an overload of client work—led me down a negative path that ended in the burnout I describe throughout this book.

Those times called for a serious empowerment chat in the mirror. Or for a little feverish journaling—*old school* style with actual pen and paper. The purpose was to remind myself of past accomplishments. For me, that meant reflecting on the fact that I'd written and self-published two books (one of which was a young adult novel called *K My Name Is Kendra* that became an Amazon Breakthrough Novel Award semi-finalist title) and an ebook. I've created training programs for administrative professionals. I've run this Virtual Assistant business of mine for over two decades—through good times and bad, for goodness' sake! These are not brags—they are confirmation that I do have the ability to finish things that I start, even if I struggle sometimes to do so.

The follow-up to that conversation with myself was a reminder that I was able to accomplish those things and more by calling on friends, family, business associates, and even experts to help me brainstorm my way through whatever block I was experiencing. It's amazing the things we forget when self-doubt kicks in and we are down on ourselves.

What about you? Are you stuck in your business planning? Have you delayed starting because you want to get *this* just right...or *that* just right...and when you do, *then* you'll be ready to move forward? Or perhaps you've started the business, but you're not getting anywhere in it because you keep planning how you will market and promote it—but you don't actually *implement* any of your ideas.

The reality, as you likely already know deep down inside, is that if you aren't careful, you'll find a way to talk yourself out of starting at all. Another day will pass, and another, and another, and months later, you will not have made any progress towards this dream you have of working for yourself in your own VA practice.

Add to all of that the trap of what we call *time-sucks.* These look different to every person, but the end result is the same: they steal our time and derail us from continuing our business journey. Spending too many hours building a website, designing a logo, setting up a professional social media presence, et cetera. These are all things you may have decided that you need for your business, but is getting these in order dragging on and on?

You may be guilty of self-sabotaging and not even realize it.

So let's get you moving forward using some or all of these simple techniques:

- **Get a brainstorming buddy!** Grab that person in your life or in your business circle who can help you talk through your ideas so you can take steps towards implementing them.

- **Don't worry about fully forming those ideas.** Use bullet points to list them, and don't worry about putting the ideas in any particular order. Just get them out of your head. You can flesh out and structure them over time.

- **Carry that list with you.** It's up to you whether you want to write them out on paper or use a note-taking app—just keep them close to you so that you can look at and add to the list whenever a new thought or idea comes to you.

- **Don't abandon any of your ideas.** The timing may not be right for some of them at that moment or at that time in your business, but you may want to revisit them later. *Sidebar: I keep all my ideas stored away in my Business Development binder. I love when I rediscover some of the good stuff I put in there months or years ago.*

- **Create timelines.** Make sure to assign dates to certain projects to determine whether you should put them out into the world now or set them aside for later.

- **Create a checklist.** I believe in the power of a good checklist. Create your own, or find inspiration in templates you find online—then tweak them to fit your personal use.

- **Amplify the power of your checklist by using it along with a digital productivity tool.** There are several: ClickUp, Trello, Monday.com, or similar platforms. These bring your checklists alive and allow you to visualize your progress in a more linear way. Index cards and a physical bulletin board in your workspace will give you the same satisfaction, if that's your preference.

The point is to get and stay unstuck when it comes to planning your business moves so that you can successfully reach the goals you've set for your VA practice. That's where a coach or mentor can be of help, as you'll read again and again throughout this book.

However you decide to move forward, just move forward. If I can do it, I know you can too!

Note it...

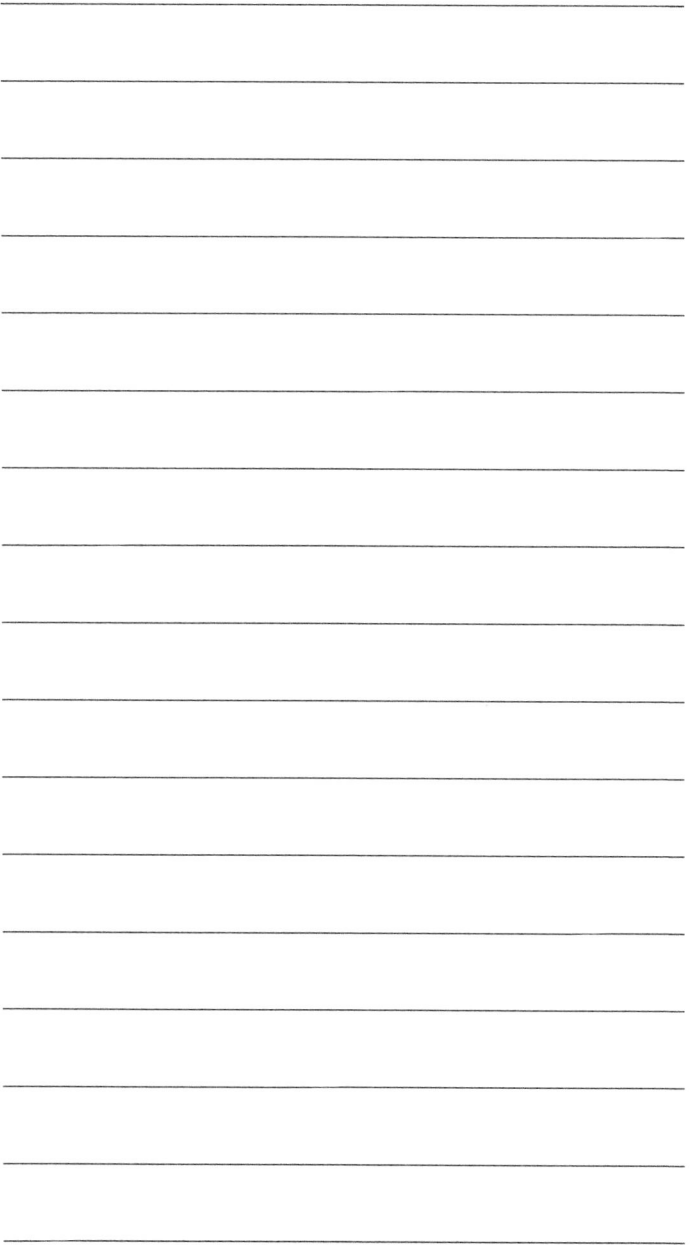

Finding Your Groove

Are you at the point in your business where you feel that you've *almost* got a good handle on everything but need a little help getting all the way there? This section will give you some useful pointers.

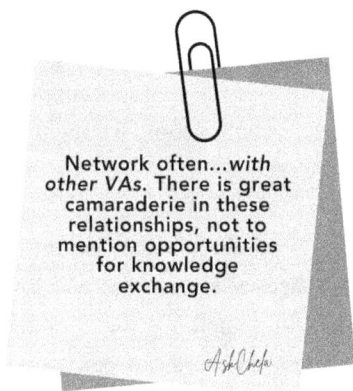

> Network often...*with other VAs*. There is great camaraderie in these relationships, not to mention opportunities for knowledge exchange.
>
> *Ask Chefa*

One of the many complaints I hear from new Virtual Assistants—and even ones who have been in business for themselves for a while but are struggling to build their practice—is that they don't have the support system around them that they feel they need to be successful. Their partners, spouses, families, and friends may not *get it*. They don't understand the industry or how anyone could possibly make a living in it (especially if the clients don't come right away), so their eyes may glaze over or roll when a VA business owner tries to explain it.

Are you experiencing this frustration right now in your journey? Are you feeling alone and misunderstood as you try to make your way through the uncertainty of getting started and, let's be honest, even stumbling a bit along the way? What can you do to build a support system around you so that you don't give up?

When I talk or write about this subject, I call it a two-step process:

- identifying and removing (or adjusting your relationship/interaction with) the often well-meaning but negative person or people around you

- replacing them with people who will cheer you on in your journey

The first step is admittedly the hardest. When is it ever easy to put space between ourselves and loved ones/friends who don't believe in something we're doing, or who don't offer up any meaningful words of encouragement when we really need it? It's uncomfortable and can be emotionally painful for reasons that are likely bigger than the situation itself.

Which is why I take my coaching clients through an exercise that involves listing their family and friends and determining the true level or lack of interest on the part of the people who matter to them. It can be quite eye-opening and can reveal allies they didn't realize they had in their corner!

Unfortunately, that's not the outcome for some VAs struggling with this issue. But, I tell them, there's an easy fix that will put you in the same "room" with people who can keep you in a positive headspace about your business: networking with other VAs on a regular basis, preferably weekly.

Camaraderie is defined as *"a spirit of trust and goodwill among people closely associated in an activity or endeavor".* I don't think there is a more fitting word to describe the sense of community you'll feel if you make it a habit to spend quality time with other VAs, which you can easily do in Facebook groups from the comfort of your own workspace and at your own convenience. Make it a point to strategically join the active ones with the goal of engaging in great conversation. About what? Business challenges, creative marketing ideas and website feedback, knowledge exchange, industry happenings, whispers and warnings, general advice and encouragement…the list goes on.

I personally love to follow up on some of my more productive interactions with fellow VAs by scheduling monthly or quarterly coffee chats with them over Zoom or Google Meet. It gives me breakroom-slash-watercooler vibes from my days as an administrative employee in Corporate America—while also helping me stay in the business-owner mindset I need to get through my workday.

Speaking of getting through the workday—working at home alone can be, well, really lonely sometimes. Pre-pandemic, I would jump in my car and change my scenery by working from a local coffee shop, the library, a rent-by-the-day single office, et cetera. But with COVID still out there, and my ongoing health issues, I am now a huge advocate of co-working with other VAs that I've met in my networking efforts. It's as simple as jumping on Zoom (or some similar platform), expressing in a few words what tasks you'll each be focusing on for the next hour or two, then muting your-selves and getting started. When appropriate, unmute your-selves to have a few minutes of chat, then re-mute and dig back in to your work. Before you know it, you're motivated and inspired to keep going and can get through what might have been a tough day.

What's also helpful about getting to know other VAs is that you come to learn *who* does *what*. It makes me think of Apple's popular *"there's an app for that"* tagline. Well, these days, there's a VA for nearly every aspect of business, and if you've made it a point to network regularly, you'll meet VAs who specialize in one skill or another that you don't. Being able to facilitate a strong referral will make you look good to a current or potential client. It'll make you *feel* good to be able to help a fellow VA. And the favor will likely be returned to you at some later date simply because you were generous of spirit.

So pull out your calendar and a notepad (yes, actually write it out by hand) to begin drafting a strategy to add this very important feature to your business development plan.

Here's one last note: *in every aspect of life, we encounter situations for which we need professional help.* We all have certain gifts, and we all have one or more areas of our life in which we have limited abilities and/or expertise. It's the same in our business lives. Sometimes we just need expert help, and there are going to come those times when all the Facebook group-ing, co-working, and networking in the world just doesn't cut it. Where do you go?

There are experts for that! As mentioned earlier in the book, get a VA coach as soon as you can. Someone who understands our unique challenges and can help you design solutions. Whether you need the occasional pump-up session or a full-fledged months-long mentor relationship, you'll want to talk to and work with someone who has been in the business for a long time, is experiencing success, and is able to help you continue moving forward in your business with practical, actionable steps.

Networking consistently with other VAs and building strategic partnerships where available and appropriate—totally worth the effort.

So get to it!

Note it...

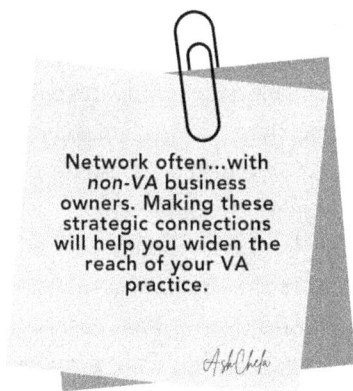

In the beginning, as you are building your business, you typically have more time to network, whether in-person or at virtual events. It is, after all, how you begin to come in contact with potential clients, or perhaps other Virtual Assistants at various points on their own entrepreneurial journey.

It's good when your efforts pay off and you land a few clients. That is the goal. But giving the bulk of your attention to your client work can sometimes leave you without any time to continue networking and making meaningful connections—and that is *not* so good. Why do I say that?

Well, the economy fluctuates, so the busy-ness of our businesses may fluctuate as well from one month or year to the next. When a recession is looming, or actually hits, clients often start looking for ways to cut their expenses, and they sometimes decide they can go back to doing some of the tasks for which they hired you, thinking they can save themselves money (usually forgetting that taking these tasks back on actually *costs* them more money, as it does not allow them to focus on the income-generating services and products they provide through their business). You suddenly find yourself scrambling to replace that lost income—and then you realize that you've not spent much time (maybe not *any* time) nurturing the connections and leads that could potentially turn into new business for you. It's a frustrating place to be on a promising VA journey.

Which is why I am encouraging you to never, ever stop networking. You're a small business owner—always remember that. As such, you'll want to spend some time each week in person or virtually with other *non*-VA business owners—and not necessarily just for the purpose of attracting them as clients. This is your opportunity to get advice on how to navigate the challenges of being in business in general (no matter the industry, product, or service), working at home alone, finding people who will cheer you on in your efforts, meeting potential clients, building your brand, marketing on a budget, et cetera.

There's just so much to discuss about *the business of being in business*, and those are much-needed conversations to have with people who actually understand the struggle. So join those Facebook, LinkedIn, and Alignable groups to have those exchanges. Find the time...no...*schedule* time to engage with the members of those groups, even if it's just for a few minutes each week. Literally block the time on your calendar so nothing else interferes with that period. Set up 15-minute coffee chats to get to know someone in another industry who has caught your professional attention online. Sign up for formal networking groups, many of whom have a structured format that allows you to introduce yourself and your business in speed-dating style one-on-one interactions with other entrepreneurs who have also invested their time and resources.

There's a science to successfully networking with other business owners. Do yourself a favor and empower yourself with a simple plan that includes this short checklist:

- Strategically choose the events you will attend or the coffee chats you set up

- Be prepared with a short description of your business and services

- Bring value to the conversations you have by actively listening and offering meaningful input

- When and where appropriate, ask thoughtful questions

- Create an elevator pitch you can use when someone shows deeper interest in what you do

- For in-person events, bring and collect business cards (or have some equally effective method in mind for keeping track of the people you meet)

- Follow up shortly after meeting by connecting on LinkedIn and/or Alignable

- Have a specific goal in mind so that you are intentional in the connections you make that day

Remember: your first goal is to build genuine relationships. Going into networking with that point of view really does take some of the pressure off and make it a more enjoyable experience for you. If you give more than you take, you might even land a client opportunity with someone looking to hire a VA for their business or make a referral to a friend who needs one.

Maintaining a presence in those circles in some small way is one of the easiest and most cost-effective ways to keep your business afloat through good times and not-so-good times. Make it a point to immediately and officially add this to your business development efforts. Trust me, you'll be glad you did.

Note it...

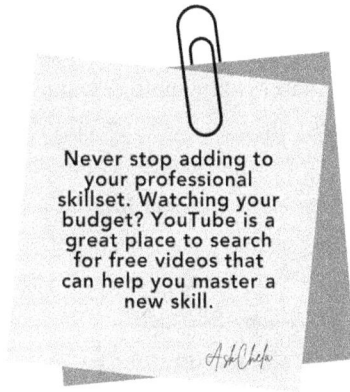

Never stop adding to your professional skillset. Watching your budget? YouTube is a great place to search for free videos that can help you master a new skill.

Ask Chloe

The responsibility of a hiring manager in a company is to oversee the opening of new positions, conduct interviews, make final decisions on who to hire, and onboard new employees. It's an important process—whether it's to bring on someone at the upper management level or someone into a key administrative role.

These professionals can tell you horror stories about the shocking number of resumes they receive for open positions, especially when searching for qualified Executive and Administrative Assistants. Literally thousands of jobseekers reply to some of the larger corporations, and hundreds to some of the smaller companies.

Given the sheer volume of applicants, which admins are they likely to choose as candidates to interview? Very likely, the ones whose resumes reflect their commitment to not only keeping up new facets of their current skill set, but who also show they are long-term or lifelong learners who seek to master new skills as opportunities to do so come along. Technology moves at warp speed, after all, and staying up-to-date with changes can benefit a company striving to grow and stand out in a competitive marketplace. Hiring team members with that same mindset is crucial to decision-makers.

Isn't that what you want for your VA practice? At the end of the day, don't you want to stand out enough that you are able to build a business that lasts for years to come? Having the best people on your team can allow you to reach that goal.

Well, if you are the sole employee of your own company, *you are the entire team*. So make an executive decision to commit yourself to staying on top of your own professional development so that you are always giving your business the best chance to succeed.

Easier said than done, Chela, you might be thinking as you review your shaky budget. *Where in the world am I supposed to find the funds for professional development?* A valid question, especially if you are at this time barely making enough money to keep your business afloat.

Here's the good news: these days, there are more and more free and low-cost courses and trainings than ever before. I always tell my coaching clients to start on YouTube. There is almost literally a video for everything, no? You probably already go there anyway for quick tutorials on how to unlock a new feature on your iPhone, cook a tasty dish for that upcoming family dinner, patch up the ripped arm of the recliner in your livingroom, learn expert ways to control your pet's anxiety, et cetera. Why not also turn there for free instructional videos related to a new business skill you want to master? A new productivity or scheduling tool that's become popular among your potential clients, for example. A course on using Canva in a bigger way. Perhaps learning how to communicate better in your business dealings, which can lead to stronger client-attracting pitches and discovery calls. Things like these can make a big difference.

It's true, of course, that you likely won't walk away from a YouTube video with a certification declaring your proficiency in a certain skill or a professional designation as a subject matter expert in your field—but it's a good start. Learn what you can at no cost, then determine what additional training or coursework you might need to pay for in order to really take things to the next level.

That next level need not cost you an arm and a leg either! Thanks to sites like Udemy, Coursera, Skillshare, LinkedIn Learning, Teachable, and many others, you can find more in-depth low-cost courses and trainings that more fully equip you as a virtual provider. This knowledge gained can empower you to offer additional and higher-end services, which translates to higher fees and more income for you. Isn't that worth a reasonable investment? As a business owner, you must remember that that is what it is: putting your money into something with potential for a profitable return.

Investing in myself and my skill set increases the value of my services and translates to more income for me. Say it over and over again out loud if you need to (I literally do that when I am considering spending certain dollar amounts in my business). And when I find myself hesitating even after having done my research, run the numbers, and documented the ways a certain professional development investment will benefit AskChela, I remember that, if added up, I likely spend that same amount on personal items I don't need: eating or drinking out, buying that cute blouse in three different colors or patterns, five different streaming services (even if they each offer something different), et cetera. You get the idea. Skipping any one of those purchases for even a thirty-day period can put money back in your pockets, which you can then invest into your business in the form of learning or honing a new income-generating skill.

I'll relate this back again to my work with authors and speakers. Overall, I have spent a few thousand dollars or more over the years on learning skills specific to those two industries so that I can offer services that my target audiences actually need. Small sacrifices have been made at times along the way—but totally worth it! Longevity is what I wanted in this career, and those investments have empowered me to meet that goal thus far. And because there are always shifts in any industry, including publishing and professional speaking, I continue to look for new and updated methods to provide services in a meaningful way to my current and prospective clients.

As with anything else, of course, going about this part of your business in an organized way will save you time and money. Keeping track of the courses you *want to* take, *should* take, *need to* take, and *have taken* will spare you the frustration of having to *research the research you've already researched*. LOL. That sentence is crazy—but you get it, no? If you don't keep a careful record of your professional development journey, then you'll spend unnecessary pockets of time trying to recall where you are on the journey. You might even mistakenly end up paying to take the exact same course more than once—a definite waste of your hard-earned resources.

When I was offering consulting to administrative employees, I found it helpful to create an actual professional development planner. Though the language mostly speaks to that role, many Virtual Assistant business owners have also found it helpful to use. You can learn more about the *AskChela Professional Development Planner for Admins* at AskChela.com.

Some closing words on this topic: *your professional development plays into your business development.* Get a good handle on both these facets of your entrepreneurial journey and you'll find it much easier to be intentional and strategic in your efforts to build a thriving VA business that lasts.

Note it...

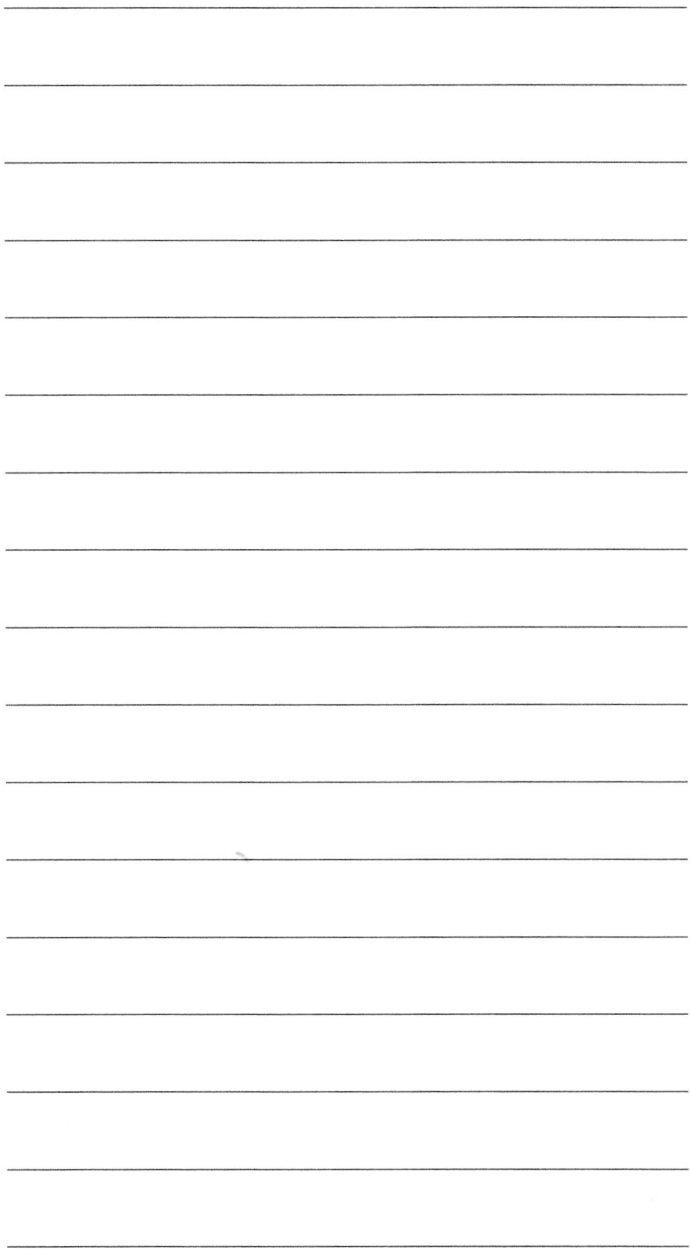

> Acknowledge your moments of self-doubt...we all have them from time to time. But don't get stuck. Take action and move beyond them.
>
> *Ash Chefa*

Confession: it's Saturday, January 13th, 2024—and I am suffering from self-doubt at this very moment as I write this chapter.

As you learned in the opening pages of this book, I literally began making notes for it as I lay in the Emergency Room dealing with resurfaced ongoing heart issues related to working too many long hours too many days of the week. I've been writing on and off for nearly a year now (*yikes*). It's not that I don't have every chapter mapped out. I do. I have for some time now. It's not that I don't know exactly what I want to say in every business lesson presented in these pages. I do. I have known for some time now.

I also know how I want to promote and market the book. I have a plan, very similar to the ones I create for my own author clients, and it includes many of the ideas I've always wanted to implement for my first nonfiction book. And I believe the book will have a measure of success, at least within my target audience. I do believe. I have always believed.

So what's the problem? What's been holding me back? Why did I stop writing just a few pages short of completing this thing? I've been asking myself the question over and over again for months now!

The answer finally came: *self-doubt*. I've battled it all my life, in personal and in business matters. And every single time I kick its butt, I am sure it won't get up to confront me again.

But it does. Every single time, even after all this time, and even after several wins and successes in my business.

Sigh.

What about you? Have you ever experienced self-doubt? Are you experiencing it right now? Is it affecting your business moves?

The truth is that most entrepreneurs—I dare say *all* of us—at some point or another experience moments of self-doubt in our journey, no matter how long we've been in business. Those moments that shake our confidence just a bit—they seem to make an appearance at the most unexpected times. Hopefully, they are infrequent and fleeting. Hopefully, we deal with them, then move on from them.

In your VA journey, you are likely going to face your fair share of self-doubt. For most VAs, it's before they start down this path. For many, it comes as they are just beginning and trying to figure their way, find their place, and stand out from the crowd. For others, it comes as they are moving along just fine in their business but suddenly land in a place of feeling unsure, even *afraid*, when the not-so-good times come along and bring financial hardship. And for still others, like me, self-doubt can come along when a life event or changes to one's health situation requires an uncomfortable shift in a typically tried-and-true business model.

Here's the good thing (and I am telling myself this as I get back to work on the book): most everything in your VA business is *figureoutable*, as Marie Forleo would say. An honest and thoughtful self-evaluation can help you take back control of whatever is happening that brought on the self-doubt in the first place. But how does one even start such an evaluation?

Use the sample statements, questions, and solutions below as examples to help you begin to think through your own personal roadblocks:

- *I am doubting myself because no one in my family or circle of friends believes in me*

Ask yourself: Why don't they believe in me? Could it be that I am showing a lack of conviction in my own abilities to start and run this business? Are my business moves unstructured and haphazard?

Figure It Out: Confidence can be contagious. If you truly believe in your ability to make your business work, and you've created and are actively implementing at least a basic business plan that feels good to you, then your confidence will shine through as you talk about your business to loved ones. Explore ways to keep that confidence level up within yourself! Network with other VAs and other small business owners. Invest in a VA coach or mentor. Do what it takes to help you take positive steps forward, even when you feel unsure. Others may see that and slowly begin to cheer you on. And even if they don't, you can be your own cheerleader if you just keep at it undeterred.

- ## *I am doubting myself because I don't have enough clients*

Ask yourself: Am I looking in the right places? Am I networking strategically...or at all?

Figure It Out: Know who your ideal client is, the services you offer that will be helpful to them, the places you can find them online, and the right approach to pitch yourself to them. Then network consistently—virtually or in-person—in the places those clients hang out. It's not always easy to put yourself out there. It can be downright uncomfortable. But the more you do it, the better you will likely become at it. Here's a tip: if you need to, find someone who can attend those events with you. A good networking buddy can boost your confidence and help you speak in a way that leads to making connections that eventually turn into clients or strategic referral partners.

- ## *I am doubting myself because I lost a client*

Ask yourself: What happened that led up to the separation? Could I have prevented it in any way? Might it actually be for the best?

Figure It Out: Take a good hard look at where things changed in your relationship with the client. Own whatever role you had in that change. Reflect on your conversations and emails with the client to determine if there were missed opportunities to communicate better. Consider your work-load and whether you took on more than you realistically should have. Be honest about whether boredom with the work played a part—perhaps causing you to not give the best level of service. And maybe, just maybe, the work and/or the client were never a good fit from the beginning. Take it as a learning experience, then move on with the goal of making your next client engagements better and stronger.

You get the idea. Rather than allowing self-doubt to settle in so deeply that it stops us dead in our tracks, take these steps instead:

- ask yourself the hard questions

- be honest with your responses

- look for the lessons to be learned from the experiences

- move on/forward to better things

You can have a successful and rewarding VA business in spite of those nasty little moments of self-doubt. Believe that fully, and you'll soon be able to navigate your way into a more positive state of mind.

Note it...

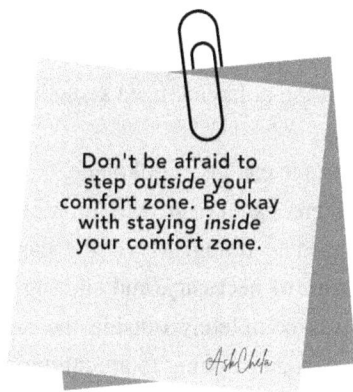

Don't be afraid to step *outside* your comfort zone. Be okay with staying *inside* your comfort zone.

Ask Chula

I have to get this off my chest: I think stepping outside one's comfort zone can be highly overrated.

Phew. Feels good to say that, especially when so many experts will tell you that you'll need to do that in order to be successful in business. In my little, humble opinion, that advice isn't necessarily the gold nugget many people think it is. For many, a valid case can be made for staying inside one's personal comfort zone.

Take me, for example. I am a woman who knows her level of comfort. In business, that means I know the types of projects and clients that make me smile, I know the ones that make me anxious, wishing I'd never taken them on, and I absolutely know the ones that make me want to run screaming into the night. Knowing that of myself, I don't typically stray too far outside my comfort zone. It's a really cozy place I've carved out for myself over time, and I like it.

Being in that place means I won't constantly be chasing my tail trying to do "all the things" in my business and potentially accomplishing none of them. It helps me avoid wasting precious time I could have been spending working at something I truly love. It lessens the likelihood of facing disappointment and failing at having tried something I didn't really want to do anyway.

The comfort zone can be a cool place.

That said, there can be growth in moving beyond the things we are used to doing. My entire career as a Virtual Assistant was born of necessity, and starting such a business back in 2001 was completely outside the norm. I'd always been an employee, so switching to an entrepreneurial mindset was a bit of a stretch, especially within an industry that hadn't really begun to be fully formed. It was a full leap of faith.

But if I'd refused to step out into the unknown, if I'd let fear completely take me over, I may not have ventured into this industry at all. If I'd stayed completely in my personal comfort zone of being employed as an Executive Assistant in Corporate America, AskChela might not even be around today. And if I hadn't, several years in, decided to niche down to working exclusively with authors and speakers (at a time when niching down wasn't really *a thing*), the trajectory of my entire administrative career might have gone completely differently.

Feel like I am giving you a mixed message? I am, it's true! And it's because this is such a debatable topic. I obviously experience conflicted feelings when someone tells me I need to step outside my comfort zone. When it's said with authority by an expert who has successfully crafted a multi-million dollar business because they took that step, it's hard to ignore.

So when I talk to my coachees about going outside their personal comfort zone, my advice instead is…maybe just step a little closer to the edge of your zone rather than jumping completely over the line. Perhaps *expand the parameters of your zone while still remaining inside it*. What does that even look like?

For me, it means *finding a balance that allows me to shine in my zone of competence* while also giving me permission and space—at my own discretion—to workshop services that aren't yet part of my main offerings but are still on-brand and have the potential to eventually become something I offer officially through my business.

On my VA journey, for instance—even as I learned how I could best support authors and speakers in their work—I quickly discovered that the most income-generating services were beyond what I was used to doing. If I was going to truly get the most out of this shift and grow my business to the point that it could sustain me financially, I was going to have to move closer to the edge of my comfort zone. I did that, taking on a client who needed someone with my background in the role of Publishing Project Manager for her hybrid publishing company. It completely changed my business for the better, as it empowered me to offer the same services to other hybrid publishers, as well as individual self-publishing authors.

Moving close to the edge of my comfort zone paid off.

So what about you? Has fear or doubt held you back from opportunities that have grown the businesses of other VAs in your circle? Maybe you regret letting these chances pass you by and, given the opportunity all over again, you would choose to step a little closer to the edge of your comfort zone —or even go completely outside of it.

It's not too late! It could make a big difference in your VA practice. But however you decide to proceed, be intentional about it. Do your research and uplevel your skill set to increase your chances of rocking out this new aspect of your business. If it works out, *yay*! That's potentially more income for you, not to mention the satisfaction that comes with doing something you love. And if it doesn't work out on the first attempt, that's okay too. Tuck it away for another time, perhaps. Maybe you'll find a way to bring it back out later. Or maybe you won't. At the very least, you will have tried and discovered that it's not for you after all. That's also part of the entrepreneurial journey.

The important thing, in my opinion, is that you don't allow someone to push you outside your comfort zone if you're not ready, not willing, or not able to be in that space. If you're going to take an uncomfortable step, do it because you truly want to. And then be strategic about it so that you have a better chance of experiencing lasting success.

Note it...

Making Boss Moves

Congratulations on rocking it out as a successful Virtual Assistant business owner! These next few tips can help you stay in the zone —even through some of the weightier decisions.

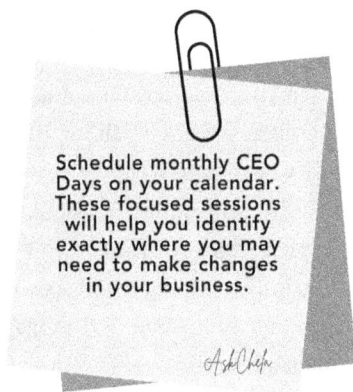

Schedule monthly CEO Days on your calendar. These focused sessions will help you identify exactly where you may need to make changes in your business.

Ask Chefe

The CEO of a company is the highest-ranking executive person in an organization. This person is in charge of day-to-day management. Depending upon the size of the company, they typically identify and drive business strategies, control how capital is allocated, determine whether to add team members, et cetera. They make the big decisions.

If you are working alone in your Virtual Assistant business, these important responsibilities fall to you, whether you actually call yourself the CEO or not. Among many other things, *you* are the one who strategizes what services you offer and how to successfully market them. *You* are the one who determines what team members, if any, are needed to maintain your business. And *you* are the one who decides how your company uses its capital with a view to maintenance and growth.

Which is why setting a CEO Day—perhaps once a month —is so important to your business. I didn't do that in the beginning, and even now I struggle to keep that appointment on my calendar. Until I realize I've missed an important marketing opportunity for one of my featured services. Or I find myself waiting until the last minute to hire another VA to help with a time-sensitive project. Or a charge for a business subscription or membership comes through and I realize that an entire month or year has passed since my last payment—and I still haven't fully utilized that particular subscription or membership! If I hadn't blown off my CEO Day, I would've been on top of all these things and been able to make informed decisions that save time and money, and head off unnecessary feelings of panic.

What does a typical CEO Day look like for me? Something like this (with coffee as needed along the way):

review of my business subscriptions

Ex. Premium LinkedIn or Alignable

Questions I ask myself:

Am I using them to my best benefit?

Or might I be able to downgrade to the free version of either or both and save money?

If I decide to keep the premium versions of either or both, what's my strategy for the next thirty days?

How does it play into my marketing?

What specific actions will I take to make sure I'm getting the most bang for my bucks?

How, specifically, will I use these tools to build my business?

review of other business subscriptions

Ex. Calendly, Office365, Adobe, etc.

Actions

If I am not actively using those and other tools like them, then I can save money by downgrading or discontinuing my subscriptions. I can always upgrade again should I need to.

review of professional organizations I belong to

Actions

If I'm not making connections or participating in a meaningful way, then perhaps now is not the ideal time for me to be a member. I can always reassess this later as I move along in my business.

If I've been smart about it, all these charges live on a budget spreadsheet: the resources I am paying for, the due date, the membership or service level, et cetera. And, of course, the column that tells me how much I am paying for each expense—with that all-important calculation at the bottom of the column that tells me the grand monthly total.

All I can say is *wow*. Seeing that total can be a real eye-opener. Getting that final number down can allow me to reinvest a few dollars back into my business in a way that can grow it.

Bringing on a team member, for instance. This was never something I imagined myself doing. I've always been content to run this operation alone. But as my service offerings shift and/or expand, and my client list grows, I realize that, if I want to keep pace with that growth (while also being mindful of my health limitations), I need help in my business, even if only from time to time, project-by-project.

So on my CEO Days, I also review and prioritize upcoming projects. If I determine I'll need help, then I spend time in my session exploring where to find that help and putting together details for the VA I engage so they can jump on the project and hit the ground running with minimal muss or fuss.

What about you? Do you have a CEO Day scheduled on your calendar? If you do, good for you! Keep it up consistently. It will definitely lead to business maintenance, if not actual measurable growth.

If you haven't yet gotten in the habit of setting aside a CEO Day, make the commitment right now to do so. Pull out your calendar, determine the best day for you (perhaps a day or two before the start of each month so you have a clear plan for the upcoming month), then block off an hour or two so nothing gets in the way.

Start with at least a regular review of your finances. Be really smart and honest with yourself in the process, including putting together a simple but solid plan to make the best use of these small investments that very quickly add up. After all, when you are a new VA—or even one who has been in business for a while—every single penny counts and can directly impact your ability to stay in business for the long haul.

Of course, there are plenty of other CEO Day tasks to consider adding in:

- organizing and cleaning up your digital desktop

- filing away any hardcopy documents

- reviewing your systems and processes (automations, sales funnels)

- marketing (creating new or tweaking old lead magnets)

- planning out the month's professional development periods

- scheduling the month's networking activities (including any coffee chats and get-to-know-you sessions)

You get the idea! Being strategic and consistent in these types of activities will help you make intelligent and informed decisions that will keep your VA practice healthy and in a constant state of growth.

Note it...

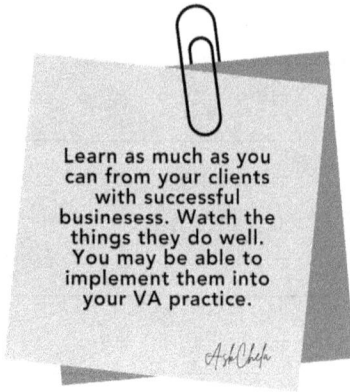

Like many kids, my first look at working was as a newspaper carrier. I learned the importance of showing up, being courteous and respectful to customers and my handler, a little bookkeeping, and a few other early life-slash-business lessons.

When I was in the tenth grade, I lost my Honor-Roll focus on my schoolwork and ended up failing two classes. I could have repeated them in my Junior year, but my father had other ideas. He not only made me go to summer school—I was required to pay for it myself. I took a job as a cashier at Burger King and, in that role, learned a lot about the importance of good customer service, teamwork, and completing tasks I didn't necessarily enjoy.

In my later teen years, I worked in a couple of offices, which gave me a glimpse into the type of work I would eventually do once I entered the workforce full-time. I became familiar with processes, honed my communication skills, observed adult teamwork at its best (and sometimes even its jaw-dropping worst...*yikes*), proper meeting etiquette, deadlines, honoring commitments, et cetera.

You see the point. In every work situation throughout my young life, I learned something that would eventually play a part in my overall career somewhere down the line in my adult life. I was appreciative of all those teachable moments even then. I didn't always like them, but I knew they were setting me up for something that would help me successfully make my way in the workplace later.

Which is why now, as a business owner, I find it so exciting to work with an assortment of author and speaker clients from a variety of backgrounds and industries. Landing a client is not just about the income—it's also about what I can learn from them. Not necessarily the ins and outs of their expertise, of course, because I could never, with my limited scope, become versed in what they've dedicated their entire careers to mastering, or what has become their life's work. And not necessarily about the projects they've hired me to consult on either. Theirs may not be that different from any other I've worked on, so there may not be much *new* to learn in that respect.

What I enjoy is *getting a more close-up view of how they've built, managed, and set their businesses up for longevity and success.* I'm interested in what tips I can pick up and implement in my own business model. I love observing how they interact with clients and other service providers. I go into the relationship with the mindset that it has the potential to be a masterclass in an area of business I've always wanted to learn.

One of my clients, for example, gave me a tip a few years ago that has served me well over time. She had already written a successful small business coaching program by the time we started working together. In encouraging me to create my own signature program, she shared with me the system she'd followed that had made the process much less daunting. She'd scheduled time with a colleague from her mastermind group, and they'd recorded themselves talking in extensive detail for hours about what she wanted to include in the program. Her Virtual Assistant transcribed the conversation, and from there she was able to pore over the notes to create an outline that would later become the Table of Contents. This approach made it much easier to begin organizing her thoughts and writing, filling in the blanks where needed, and pulling quotes from her own words that could also be repurposed in her marketing. She used this same process for writing several books.

I followed her example in putting together a training program for administrative professionals a few years ago. And this book you're reading right now is a result of that same technique.

Another client I supported runs a highly successful membership site. I'd always wanted to start one of my own, but had no idea how to even get started. Working with her gave me an inside view of the set-up and management of such a site, which, in turn, gave me the confidence to take another step towards creating my own upcoming membership site.

One other client—a colorful, pull-no-punches marketing professional from Boston——engaged me to help write a strategic plan for a client of hers. I'd never done one before, and I was more than a little hesitant to take on the challenge. Her response to my hemming and hawing? *"You're a good writer, Chela. Get over yourself. You can do this."*

So I did it, and she liked my work enough that the door was left open to join her on other such projects. Additionally, it gave me the confidence to add a similar service to

AskChela for indie and self-published authors in need of marketing assistance.

If I hadn't had the chance to roll up my sleeves and gain hands-on experience by working closely with these three amazing women (my ideal client types, by the way), I may not have found the courage to make boss moves in my business. That's a lesson I have learned over and over again.

I'm encouraging you to do the same when you have a discovery call with a prospective client. Look at each relationship as an opportunity for you to not just earn money, but also to learn:

- what successful processes look like

- what you might do differently to achieve better or different results in your own business

- what not to do at all...*ever*

Use whatever bit of knowledge you gain to help you hone your skill set, build your confidence, develop techniques that feel comfortable to you, and grow your business overall. The value of what you learn while working with such clients can change everything.

Note it...

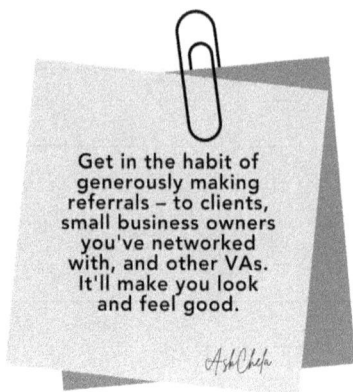

> Get in the habit of generously making referrals – to clients, small business owners you've networked with, and other VAs. It'll make you look and feel good.
>
> *AskChela*

In my work with authors and speakers, I'm often running in the same circles as some of my favorite creative types: artists, illustrators, interior book designers, photographers, cover designers, proofreaders, editors, writing coaches, hybrid publishers, et cetera. Their gifts are not my gifts, and vice versa, so when a client is in need of a service provider whose talents are beyond mine, I love to be able to make a referral. It makes me look good, feel awesome, and aligns with the AskChela brand, which by name alone implies that if someone needs my services, I'll either be able to provide them myself or point the person in the direction of a reputable resource.

Knowing the benefits of making *authentic* connections with people who can help me make my clients happy is key to my personal networking strategy. It helps me go into a business setting, not necessarily with the goal of pitching my services to get new clients, but open to the idea of meeting people who can then become part of my referral universe. At the end of the day, it still benefits my business and can ultimately be as income-generating as having landed a paying client, as new connections may have colleagues who are in need of the specific set of services I offer.

I always recommend to my coaching clients and mentees that they get in the habit of building their own referral network in order to be prepared for this very situation. And I'm passing it along to you because I see it as a major part of your business development efforts.

A word of caution here, of course: *do your homework before putting your own reputation on the line by making a referral.* Take time to get to know the person as best you can before connecting them with someone who trusts your recommendation!

In this scenario, I like to relate it back to Corporate America. Let's say you're working for a respected company where you've built up a good reputation for yourself in the hallways and conference rooms as a hardworking, thoughtful employee that can be trusted to get the job done thoroughly and on-time. Your work ethic eventually leads to your being offered a promotion, which then leaves your current role open. Human Resources wants to know if you have a friend you can recommend as your replacement. You don't have to offer up a candidate—but you'd love to, if at all possible, because you kind of want to be the hero in this situation by helping them move through the hiring process quickly.

Would you recommend someone you've just met in passing? Someone you shook hands with once as you took their business card, but whose name you barely know, not to mention their skill set and capabilities? Again, your personal reputation, your well-respected *word* is on the line. What do you do?

You may be presented with a similar situation as a business owner. You find that you are unable to take on a certain client or project, but you've made a solid enough impression on the person inquiring about your services that they feel comfortable asking if you wouldn't mind making a referral to someone who can assist them. You like them, you don't want to let them down, and you want to look good in their eyes in case there is a possibility for you to work together in the future. What do you do?

This very scenario is one of the reasons I teach my coachees to make getting to know other service providers, both inside *and* outside of the virtual assistant world, a priority in their business development strategy. Make real, authentic connections so you can build a referral network that benefits you and those within it.

I mentioned doing homework. What might that include? A visit to their website, to start. And if they don't have a website, I expect that, as a service provider, they have some other sort of online presence that speaks to the services they offer. Before I am able to make a recommendation, I'll want to see samples of their work (in the case of a cover designer or typesetter, for instance), or praise from happy clients. I'd love to see a bio as well, as it may tell more of that person's story, as well as their professional affiliations (i.e. an editor being a member of the Editorial Freelancers Association). Social media posts can be rather revealing, so if they include on their website any icons to these profiles, I briefly scroll through these as well. All of this *recon*, as I call it, gives me a sense of their skill set, as well as a bit of insight into their personality. If I'm particularly excited about what they do and how it might benefit a current or prospective AskChela client, I reach out to set up a coffee chat to get to know them better over Zoom or Google Meet.

I don't do so to pass judgment on this person. I am doing

it for the benefit of everyone involved so that none of us are wasting precious-slash-billable time and/or resources, or risking our reputations unnecessarily in small business circles because of not having done our due diligence. If it can happen to million-dollar corporate brands and organizations who then see a downturn in their profits because of a risky alliance (or even just the *appearance* of such an alliance), it can certainly happen to a small business and be far more devastating.

And here's one thing I know for sure: anyone who has ever referred business to AskChela has taken these same steps before introducing their connections to me. I don't take offense at that.

So get busy making authentic connections. Systematically build it into your business development efforts. Before you know it, you can find yourself with a VA practice that is mostly propped up by solid referrals. That's a really good place to be on any business journey.

Note it...

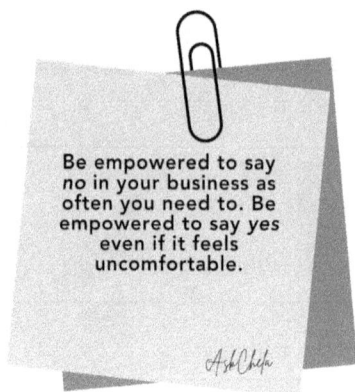

Sprinkled throughout this book is advice about trying to only take on clients or projects that you enjoy, that give you inner calm and a sense of purpose—along with income, of course. That is easier said than done, I admit. Depending upon where you are in your business, your biggest concern is likely landing whatever clients you can. I get that.

But there will likely come a time or two when you're not quite sure you should take on a particular client or project. Perhaps you feel completely unqualified. Or you really don't like the work they would like to hire you to do. Or you sense immediately that the client's personality just doesn't click with yours to the degree that it will be problematic. For whatever reason, you don't think working with them is a good fit.

It's okay to say *no* to the opportunity.

That is the beauty of working for yourself. You are the boss. you are in control of who you choose to work with.

It's okay to say *no*.

I've done that more than once in my career as a Virtual

Assistant. In fact, I did it shortly before wrapping up the writing of this book. For reasons that made sense to me at the time, and after careful consideration, I turned down potential work that had come to me by referral. I took the meeting out of a sense of gratitude, but I was convinced after getting all the details that it just didn't seem a good fit for me. I liked the owners of the company, I liked their message, I liked their business model, and I liked the person who had made the referral. I just didn't feel confident that I could perform the work because it wasn't something I was comfortable with and it was outside of what I typically love to do. I walked away from the opportunity.

I'm certainly not the first VA to have done that. In fact, you may someday find yourself making the same decision in your business. What that does is leave room in your schedule to pursue opportunities you really like. Presented skillfully, your *no* also gives you a chance to show that prospective client your level of professionalism—that you care about doing a good job, you care about the integrity of their business and yours, and that you don't feel you'll be able to deliver what they need in a way that will benefit them. You really don't need to go into any more detail than that. You're the decision-maker in this scenario, so that explanation should suffice.

As I said in the previous lesson—what you can do, if it makes sense and seems appropriate, is offer to make a referral to someone you feel *can* handle the project. If you've been networking and getting to know other VAs all along, you may be able to make a connection that will benefit everyone involved: you'll potentially look good for the recommendation, the VA you refer (with their permission) may gain a new client, and the business owner will get their work completed. Win-win.

Now, there's always a case to be made for the other side of the coin, of course: saying *yes*, even if it feels a bit uncomfortable. You might decide to do so because, well, you really do need the work. Or the prospective client's task will allow you to learn something you've always wanted to know and will help you build your skill set, which could lead to a new service you can offer to others. Or you just really like the person and want to work with them.

That has absolutely happened to me before, as I have alluded to a couple of times in this book. In fact, the business owners I mentioned a couple of paragraphs ago—we're now working together! After further consideration, I decided that I really wanted to learn the role for which they were seeking to hire a VA after all. In my head, I realized it would ultimately benefit my business to add this work to my skill set. I reached back out to the company, and after a few weeks, the opportunity for us to have a second discussion opened up. We decided to move forward.

I'll be honest—it didn't start out well. I am used to rocking out any role I take on, because I only take on the roles I can rock out. It's the comfort zone thing. But when I started out in this role, I found myself in the uncomfortable position of *not* rocking it out immediately, and I didn't like that feeling at all. I had pretty much decided to make a quick exit before I embarrassed myself more than I already felt that I had, but I changed my mind and wrote a sincere email to my clients to express how lost I felt in the work. We had a meeting to chat it out, and decided on a corrective course that we all agree empowered me to make speedy progress. I still have lots to learn, but I feel much more comfortable now.

The point? It is indeed okay to say *yes* to an opportunity even if that inner voice is whispering otherwise. As we talked about in an earlier lesson—stepping closer to, or outside of, the edges of your personal comfort zone might be a game-changer for you. As a small business owner, you're empowered to make that decision for yourself.

If you're leaning towards a *yes* but your hesitation is that you don't feel you have the complete skill set needed, be sure to be transparent with the client about your abilities in this unfamiliar territory. Let them decide whether they want to take the chance on bringing you to their team. And if you do end up taking on the client, commit to rocking it out fully for as long as you are in the role.

But what do you do if you ultimately discover that you should have listened to that cautionary whisper all along? For whatever reason, you decide you'd rather not continue working with the client. Perhaps it no longer makes sense to do so. Perhaps the workload is no longer sustainable. Or perhaps you even determine that it is literally *unhealthy* for you to continue the working relationship itself. What do you do? What do you say? How do you bow out gracefully while also maintaining a level of professionalism?

Being prepared ahead of time is key, because the reality is that things change. People change. Circumstances change. As entrepreneurs, we have to be ready to deal with those changes and keep moving forward. It's the reason we put carefully worded language—and even official legal clauses—in the contracts we sign with our clients. Things change, and these documents protect everyone involved when that happens.

What we are not always prepared for is how it feels *emotionally*. It isn't typically easy to walk away from a professional situation we had hoped would work out. Honestly, there are times that it literally hurts and keeps you awake at night. But personal experience has taught me: *listen to that voice when it's time to move on from a client.* Try really hard not to leave them in a lurch if you can help it—but listen to that voice! What you don't want to happen is that you let a situation go on and on for so long that it begins to affect your wellbeing—physically, mentally, or otherwise. What you don't want is for your mindset to take such a hit that your work suffers. That will only make things worse, and it can affect the health of your business from the inside out. It's hard to operate from such a negative space, as it can cause you to lose your confidence. A loss of confidence can spiral into so much more.

Believe it or not, I've been there.

The decision to accept or decline an opportunity in your business is all yours. Whatever you do, do yourself a favor and give each opportunity the careful consideration it demands. Study it from every angle to determine how it will affect you personally and professionally. Make your decision and commit to it either way—but be unapologetically empowered to make whatever adjustments you may need to in order to be successful on your journey.

Note it...

Don't be afraid to
make a shift in your
business (or even
completely reinvent it)
if it no longer serves
you the way you want
it to.

Ask Chefa

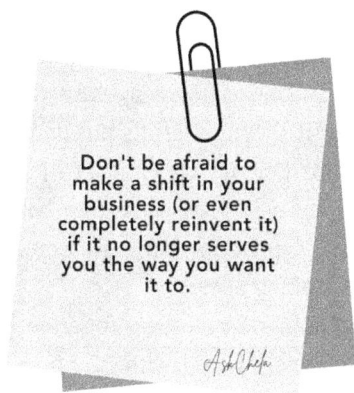

As you read in the opening pages of this book and throughout, I completely stumbled into the world of virtual assistance. I didn't have a plan, I didn't have a support system, I didn't have a business model. I just knew that I needed to find a way to work, even in the midst of a challenging economy. Offering to small businesses the same administrative tasks I'd always performed in Corporate America just made sense to me and seemed the easiest route. So that's how I marketed my services in the beginning.

After a few years, I decided it just wasn't enough. I was not enjoying my business. It was almost just as mind-numbing as the work I'd been doing as an administrative employee since the age of fifteen. I wanted more.

Once I learned a few years in that I could work with authors and speakers offering services beyond the general tasks I'd become bored with, everything changed. And so I reinvented my business to match my creative interests and serve me the way I needed it to at that time. Thank goodness, because I'm not sure I'd be in this industry today, years and years later, if I hadn't made that change.

Are you still in the research phase of starting a career as a Virtual Assistant? This lesson may help take a little bit of stress off of you. Knowing that it's not unusual for someone in our industry to start out one way and then shift or niche down to a different set of services—maybe even a different ideal client—can be empowering as you start your own journey and are looking ahead.

Have you been in your business for a few years and found that you are absolutely bored with it? Maybe it just doesn't feel the same as it did when you first started out—doesn't give you the same satisfaction or buzz. Perhaps you're a different person than you were when you first began. Or the original purpose of being in business for yourself has changed over time. It might be time to reinvent your business to fit the *you* you are *right now*.

A regular assessment of your business is extremely helpful in this regard. It will alert you to changes that you might need or want to make, even if those changes cannot happen until a future date. Perhaps these assessments are timed quarterly as part of one of your CEO Day sessions. Maybe twice a year works best for you, or even annually. I love a good annual review, because it gives me a wider snapshot of what worked well throughout the year before—and what didn't.

Perhaps your business serves you differently over the summer months (maybe you're traveling more and want to unplug for a few weeks to rejuvenate) than it does over the winter period. Or you're a mom whose business needs change based on whether the kiddies are in school or not. You may find it useful to shift as you need to in order to address those times of the year.

Reinvention can be fun. It can keep things fresh and exciting throughout what you hope will be a longtime career. Famous creatives do it all the time! In the early days of their careers, they may wear meat dresses to red carpet events, then after some time appear in tastefully elegant sequined gowns alongside superstar crooners (I'm looking at you, Gaga). Reinvention can lead to much-deserved growth.

Whatever your situation, the lesson is that you don't have to be stuck to the same model you had when you started out, or even the one you had six months ago. *You are the one building the model* after all, and can change it as you see fit to address your specific needs at any given time. It is completely up to you. It is your superpower. Own it!

This is where that vision board I suggested earlier comes into play. If things seem a little stale in your business right now, that vision board can spark new ideas that excite you. If you've kept adding to it over time, you might find buried somewhere under all the pinned ideas that one idea that would change everything in your business. Or if a vision board is not your style, try keeping a box full of your ideas. I found a pretty hat box I like, and I call it my Box of Big Ideas. It's full of half-ideas (which I technically don't yet know are actually *big* ones, but whatever) scribbled on scraps of paper and small index cards. From time to time, when I'm feeling bored in my business, I go through that box to see what forgotten gems might be in there. Perhaps a digital download I thought once about creating, a new service I'd like to try out, or a quick tutorial I want to record and share with my coaching clients. Maybe even a workshop idea I want to flesh out more fully.

Whatever the degree of the shift, be strategic about it. Ask yourself a few key questions so that you don't find yourself going so far off course that you lose your place or waste precious time in your business. Give these some thought:

- Do I understand why I feel the need to make this change at this time?

- How will it affect my immediate and current workload?

- How will it affect my client list?

- Am I making this change on a whim or out of emotion?

- How committed am I to seeing it through?

- Do I have the ability to do what is required for this change?

- What processes will I need to put into place to help sustain this change?

The point is to *design a business that works for you however you need it to work for you for as long as it needs to work for you.* That's at the core of every good business development plan—and it's the dream of every entrepreneur who has ever decided to take this crazy journey.

Note it...

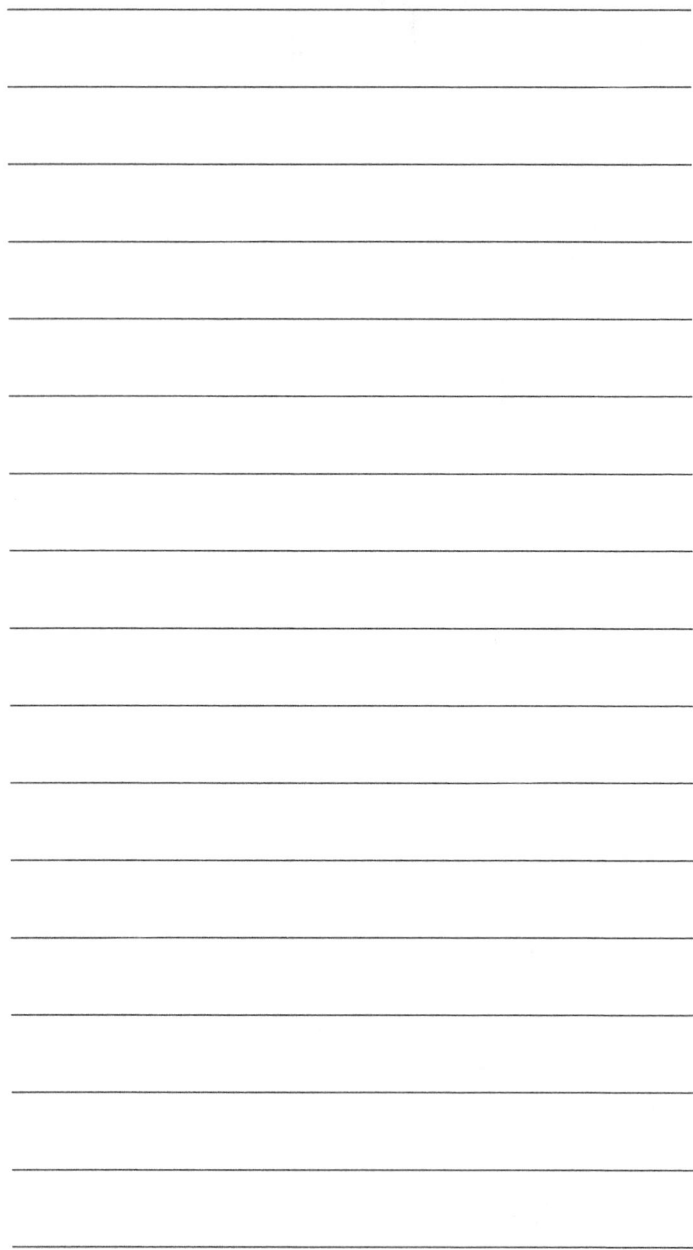

If you have to put your business on any reason, stay connected to the VA industry and community. It can help you make your way back when the timing is better.

Ask Chefa

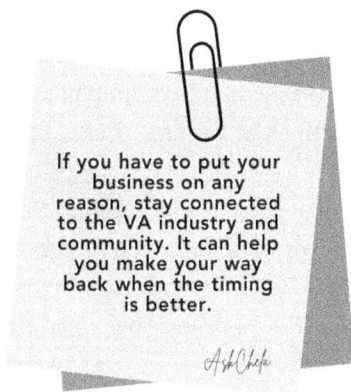

Starting a business is not nearly as hard as *staying* in business. That's where the real effort comes in. You may already have discovered this yourself if you've launched and have been diligently trying to build your Virtual Assistant practice for some time.

The reality is that not everyone is going to be successful in their venture. It usually isn't for lack of trying, because most people are willing to put in the work. The cold, hard truth is that sometimes the timing is off, or self-doubt and overwhelm kick in and stay too long, or a lack of emotional support from the people closest to you begins to take its toll after a while. You may find yourself unmotivated, stuck in a negative mindset you can't shake off, and wondering if you should just shut it all down and walk away.

I know most of those feelings very well, even after two decades of doing this. But I always stop short of wondering if I should walk away, because I know that's not the answer. I've known that since the very beginning, back in 2001, when

I set out on this journey without a map to guide me, and without the amazing community of virtual professionals that exists today. I knew that what I'd gotten myself involved in was special and had merit and exciting possibilities, even if it wasn't clearly defined at the time. I could feel it deep down inside.

I also knew that I needed an income! So my VA journey includes periods of time that found me back at a desk working in Corporate America to support myself. It wasn't ideal, considering I'd more than once had a taste of what it would be like to work for myself, empowered to choose the types of clients and projects that appealed to me. It was *hard*. I wanted so much to get back to doing work as what had finally come to be known as *virtual assistance*. I wanted to be out there helping the industry take shape and form.

In my full-time Corporate America roles, I couldn't do that. I couldn't devote much time and energy to building my VA practice. But what I *could* do was watch how the industry was developing. I could take notes from the thought leaders who were setting standards and making names for themselves. And I could certainly retain a small client or two to keep my entrepreneurial fire stoked. I had every intention, after all, of making my way back to the growing industry as a full-time business owner. That's what kept me going.

What about you? Are you at a point in your journey where you're questioning your decision to follow this path? What if you find that the best decision, at least for now, is to pause your business and go back to working a traditional 9 to 5 position?

If that is what makes sense, I really want you to keep this advice in mind:

- **Stay connected** in some way to the industry and your business. Subscribe to free VA newsletters, make it a point to follow and read blogs (or watch YouTube videos) that keep you up to date on current trends in our industry.

- **Facebook** is an awesome place to connect and engage with other VAs, typically at no cost to you. Join active groups, interact by making comments on posts that interest you, follow or send friend requests to other VAs whose vibe you like.

- Follow VA content on **Instagram** too! Again, engage with posts you find interesting, even if you're just "liking" them. Take note of the comments on those posts to see what encouragement and/or tips you can pull from there as well, especially if those posts resonate with you in some way.

- If **TikTok** is your thing, regularly check out the movers and shakers there. They tend to be younger and a bit more willing to explore new ideas for building their VA careers and attracting clients, which might be fun to watch if you're looking to refresh your business when you return to it.

- **LinkedIn**, in my opinion, is key to maintaining a professional presence, whether as an employee or a small business owner. If you don't have a profile there, set one up—then be sure to keep it active by joining groups (VA *and* small business), making connections, subscribing to newsletters, attending free virtual business events, et cetera.

- **Alignable** is an amazing platform for small business owners. Set up your free profile there, then follow the same formula as you do for LinkedIn. Their connection process is a bit different on the free level, so be very strategic about how you network there.

- If you have a **website** up but don't plan to maintain it, then perhaps take it down so that it doesn't look dated. But keep your domain name active! You don't want to lose your brand identity, especially if you've figured out what that identity is.

You get it. The point is to stay present, connected, and up-to-date on current trends in our industry and in the business world at large so that you don't find yourself so far behind those trends when you return that it makes your comeback—if you're planning to make a comeback—any more challenging than it will already be.

Note it...

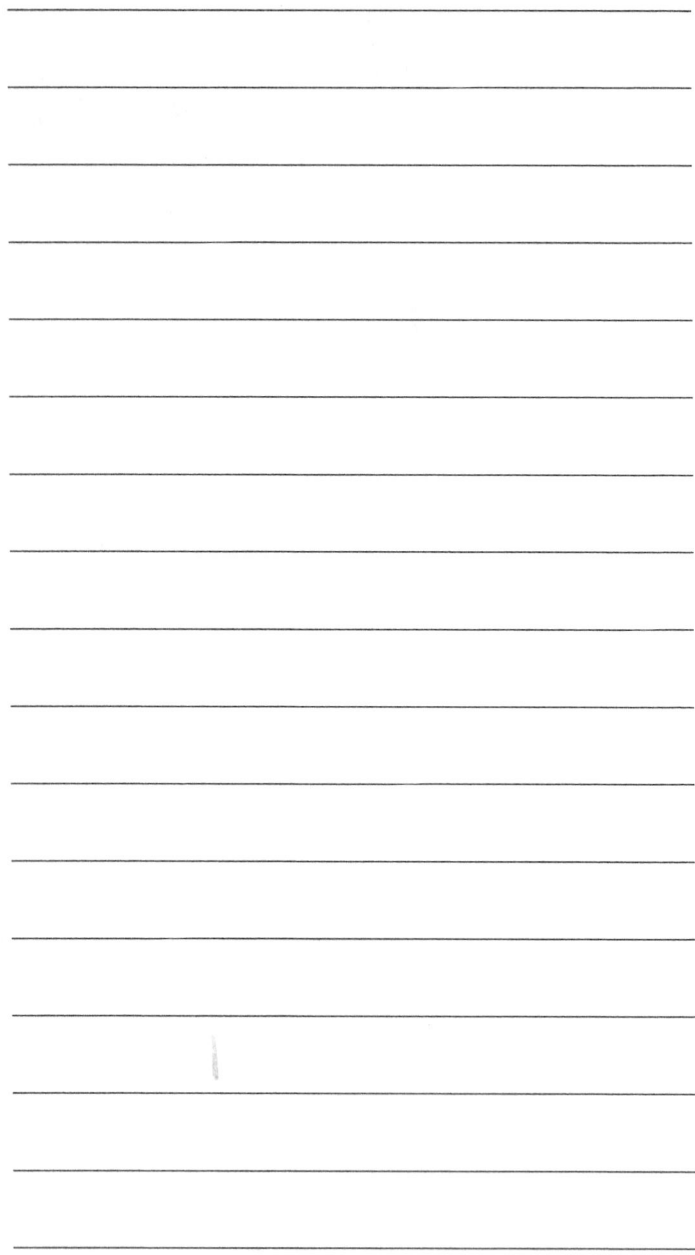

Parting Thoughts

Please take care of yourself...

> Take self-care and health breaks seriously. It's hard to run your business at its best if you don't set aside and take the time to rest your mind and body.
>
> *AskChefa*

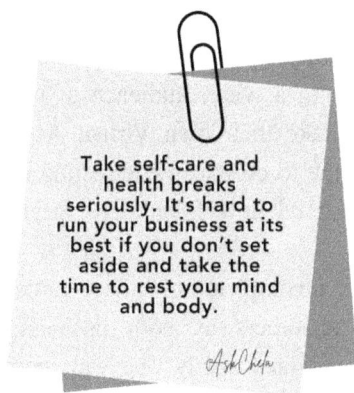

Wow. It's finally done.

Writing this book has been a true labor of love. It has been cathartic. And it has been a necessary reminder to myself to take my own self-care seriously. To get back to my daily naps, to my lower-stress lifestyle, to my mental health breaks as needed. I cannot, after all, deliver rockstar quality work to my clients if I'm not well myself. And as I wrote this book over the course of a year following a resurgence of my health issues, I have to admit that I had been unwell for several months leading up to my hospital visits and medical leave from my business. I realize now that I had been completely immersed in *grind culture*—that toxic state of being in which I felt the need to hustle all the time. To rarely be unavailable, even on nights and weekends. To never stop going until I'd used up every single moment of every single day. You know where that lands you? On the dark side, exactly where I was a year ago.

But I am a silver-lining kind of woman, and there is definitely one to this story! That downtime gave me quiet moments to jot down various thoughts that had been swimming around in my mind for years. Thoughts I'd always wanted to share to a wider audience of professionals who had decided to take their own Virtual Assistant journey. I had plenty of time to do that while resting up and reflecting on my situation and how I had let everything get out of control.

My random, incomplete notes have turned into lessons I can offer up to others as both business advice and a cautionary tale of how easily one can ignore the warning signs of working too much and find themselves off-balance.

So here are a few tips for designing with intention a business balanced with work, proper rest, and relaxation:

- Enjoy your weekends and personal periods of downtime

- Create and/or follow a calendar that allows you to periodically close your business and be completely unavailable to clients

- Schedule/take occasional Mental Health Days

- Get up from your desk and go for walks, even if only for a few minutes to get some fresh air and clear your head

- Hang out with the ones you love

Oh my goodness, this list could go on and on, no? I hope you feel that way too, and I hope you'll use the note pages at the end of this section to jot down those things that make you smile, relax your mind, and bring you calm. That's what moments of self-care are supposed to do.

Ahhh…

That said, I have to tell you one huge thing I've reintroduced into my life that gives me all the feels I'd been missing for so long: Reggie Brown is back! You remember—the little fictional character I told you about in Lesson 8. As I say in my marketing materials: she's back, she's still nine-years-old, and she's still *too much*.

I never meant to tuck her away for so long. *You're Too Much, Reggie Brown* was always supposed to lead to a series of books, and as I made appearances promoting it, I spoke about it as a series. It just never happened. Life got in the way, as it often does. And *business* writing is what pays the bills.

Very recently, though, I opened up my Reggie Brown files, dusted off my notes and news clippings, and decided to dive back into writing her story. Only this time, I decided, she needs to have a bigger purpose. She won't just live in the pages of books. I want this kid to become the icon of literacy that I had always envisioned her to be, most especially within inner city communities and school systems. So, in addition to planning a relaunch of the original book with new cover art, I've also created classroom activities that will get her in front of educators who I hope will incorporate her into their third, fourth, and fifth grade curriculum. The possibilities are endless!

But even if that doesn't happen—because, well…*Life*—I will definitely keep writing Reggie Brown stories because there is still an audience of fans out there, and knowing that makes me happy. Writing these stories makes me smile, relaxes my mind, and brings me calm.

Please commit to finding the self-care moments that work

for you. Honor them by interjecting them into your work life. It will keep you in a better place mentally and emotionally, which can help you stay in and enjoy your business for years to come.

That's the biggest lesson of all.

Note it...

Get the Workbook

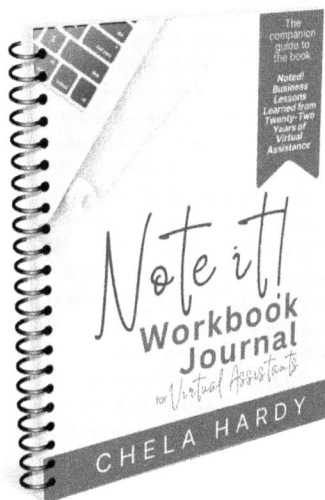

This companion to ***Noted! Business Lessons Learned from Twenty-Two Years of Virtual Assistance*** features worksheets, writing prompts, activities and exercises designed to help VAs think through and move beyond some of the common roadblocks that may be hindering their professional growth and the health of their business.

Available for purchase and download exclusively at
AskChela.com

Grab this Ebook

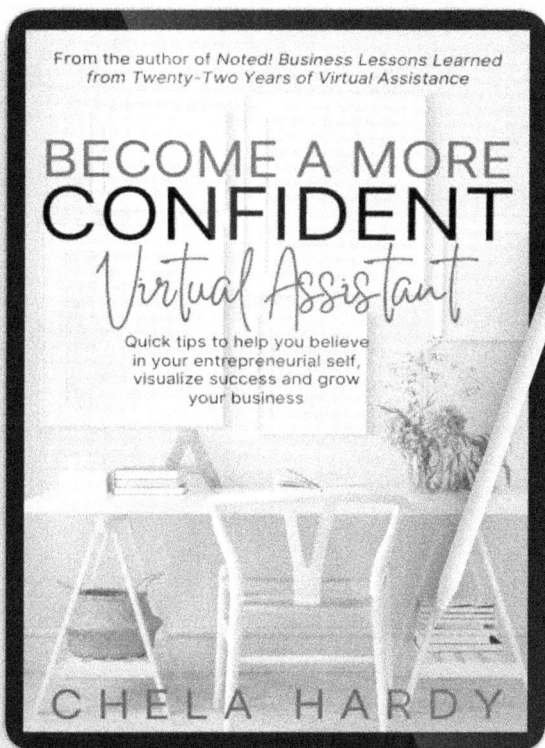

From the author of *Noted! Business Lessons Learned from Twenty-Two Years of Virtual Assistance*

BECOME A MORE
CONFIDENT
Virtual Assistant

Quick tips to help you believe in your entrepreneurial self, visualize success and grow your business

CHELA HARDY

This quick read offers up five ways to easily put a plan in place to boost your confidence and move you forward in your career goals.

Buy now on Amazon.com

More from AskChela

VIRTUAL ASSISTANT Q&A

Thinking of becoming a Virtual Assistant? Need more information in order to decide if it's the right career path for you? Confused about how to get started? Schedule an affordable 45-minute one-on-one session and let's get your specific questions answered.

VA BIZ BRAINSTORM

Already in business but not having the success you'd hoped for? In a one-on-one 45-60 minute session, let's brainstorm some ideas to see where you might need to make changes to your client-attracting efforts.

30-DAY VA SUCCESS MINDSET COACHING

Aligning yourself and your business with a healthy mindset is a key component in the formula for success. Let's focus on retraining your brain to meet that challenge with a personal assessment, a determination of realistic goals, and a simple action plan to implement your strategies in a way that feels comfortable to you.

* * *

Visit the website for more info on our mentoring program and monthly subscription access to *Chela's BizDev Binder for Virtual Assistants*.

About the Author

Chela Hardy is a former Executive Assistant who transitioned into a career as a Virtual Assistant (VA) in 2001. Since 2013, she has shared her industry knowledge as an instructor teaching an Adult Ed course on how to start and successfully run a home-based VA business. She's the creator of **Chela's BizDev Binder for Virtual Assistants** and the founder of **AskChela.com**, where she blogs about the industry and offers coaching and mentoring services to VAs at every stop on their journey. Chela delivers creative services and publishing project management through her website **AuthorAndSpeakerServices.com**. Also known as Kamichi Jackson, she is the author of *K My Name is Kendra* (an Amazon Breakthrough Novel Award semi-finalist title) and *You're Too Much, Reggie Brown*, and is the creator of Reggie Reads, a classroom program for elementary school readers.

LinkedIn
https://www.linkedin.com/in/chelahardy
Alignable
https://www.alignable.com/winterville-nc/askchela-llc
Facebook
https://www.facebook.com/chelamhardy
Instagram
https://www.instagram.com/askchela

157

Interviews

SEASON 2, EPISODE 2

UP CLOSE AND VIRTUAL PODCAST
Host: Katie Tew

with guest Chela Hardy of AskChela

TUNE IN AT WWW.SPOTIFY.COM

EPISODE 54

BUSINESS STORIES OF SUCCESS PODCAST
Host: Marc Adams

with guest Chela Hardy of AskChela

TUNE IN AT BUSINESS50SPODCAST.COM

EPISODE 606

THE WRITE COACH PODCAST
Host: Joyce Glass

with guest Chela Hardy of AskChela

TUNE IN AT WWW.THEWRITECOACH.BIZ/606/

Featured Articles